Milo B. Price

Teutonic Antiquities in the Generally Acknowledged Cynewulfian Poetry

Milo B. Price

Teutonic Antiquities in the Generally Acknowledged Cynewulfian Poetry

ISBN/EAN: 9783337220020

Printed in Europe, USA, Canada, Australia, Japan

Cover: Foto ©Thomas Meinert / pixelio.de

More available books at **www.hansebooks.com**

TEUTONIC ANTIQUITIES
IN THE GENERALLY ACKNOWLEDGED
CYNEWULFIAN POETRY.

A DISSERTATION

PRESENTED TO THE PHILOSOPHICAL FACULTY

OF THE

UNIVERSITY OF LEIPZIG

FOR THE ACQUISITION OF THE DEGREE

OF

DOCTOR OF PHILOSOPHY

BY

M. B. PRICE.

LEIPZIG
PRINTED BY ERNST HEDRICH.
1896.

CONTENTS.

INTRODUCTION	1
I. MYTHOLOGY	5
II. RELIGIOUS CONCEPTIONS .	9
1. God and Christ	9
2. The Holy Spirit and the Trinity .	16
3. Virgin Mary	18
4. Heaven	19
5. Angels	22
6. Devil	25
7. Hell .	29
III. THE STATE .	33
1. Ruler . .	34
2. Ruled . .	38
3. Punishment . .	42
4. War and Warriors . . .	44
5. Domestic and other Relations .	49
IV. NATURE	58—65

INTRODUCTION.

I present in the following pages the result of a study of the acknowledged Cynewulfian poems with reference to their Teutonic Antiquities. The fact that Anglosaxon poetry, even when based upon and closely following a Latin source, has a large element of native material which contributes in no small degree to a correct knowledge of the life and thought of the people themselves is generally recognized. Several pains-taking investigations have brought into clearer light the genuinely Teutonic side of a number of the longer Anglosaxon poems; among others that of Schultze, Altheidnisches in der angelsächsischen Poesie, speciell im Beowulfliede, Berlin 1877, and of Köhler, Alterthümer im Beowulfliede, Germania XIII, 129 ff., of Rau, Germanische Alterthümer in der Angelsächsischen Exodus, Leipzig, 1889, and of Kent, Teutonic Antiquities in Andreas and Elene, Leipzig 1887 and of Ferrell, Teutonic Antiquities in the Anglosaxon Genesis, Leipzig, 1893.

To make this presentation of the Teutonic aspect of the recognized Cynewulfian poetry complete it has been necessary for me to incorporate considerable material respecting the Elene in the essay, which has already been sought out and discussed by Mr. Kent in his dissertation upon Andreas and Elene. The inclusion of the Elene in the study has its justification only in the greater completeness of the presentation as I do not flatter myself to have found much in addition to what Mr. Kent has presented, however my views may differ from his on some minor points. But the omission of the Elene in a discussion treating this aspect of the Cynewulfian poems would leave the presentation most incomplete; for where in Cynewulf's literature are those favorite topics of the Anglosaxon poet, war-and sea-life, so vividly presented as in Elene?

Respecting those poems which are based upon Latin homilies or legends, those naturally yield the most to the end in view which are most lax in the use of their source, while those that follow an original most scrupulously yield less of interest for our purpose. Crist, Juliana, Guthlac B and Elene are all based, to a greater or less extent, upon earlier Latin writings. Gregory's X and XXIX homilies and the Vulgate were freely used in Crist (cf. also Prof. Cook, Modern Language Notes of America, IV, 171 ff., respecting the relation of the hymn De die Judicii to the third part of Crist. Juliana is based upon the legend of St. Juliana, which is found in the Acta Sanctorum, Feb. 16th Vol. II. 873—877; Guthlac B follows the Vita sancti Guthlaci of Felix of Croyland, Acta Sanctorum, Apl. 11th, Vol. II. p. 48ª — 50ᵇ, and Elene follows, with a considerable degree of exactness, the vita Quiriaci¹), Acta Sanctorum, May 1th, I, p. 445ᵇ – 448. All of these poems are ecclesiastical in general and do not therefore offer the wealth of secular information that many Anglosaxon poems afford; yet we shall see that even in Crist, which "of all the Old English poems is that which reveals in the most complete and effective manner the spirit of Christianity and christian Latin poetry"²), there are slight traces of mythology and passages decidedly heathen in their coloring.

The conservative reactionary movement of criticism in recent years respecting what poems *are* the work of the bard Cynewulf and what ones have been falsely attributed to him, I take it, warrants the use, in an essay designing to treat Cynewulfian poems alone, of only one poem, Guthlac B, in addition to those about whose authorship the poet's own signature leaves no room for doubt. Whether or not the Anglosaxon Riddles, or a part of them, are to be attributed to Cynewulf, is still an unsettled question. The consensus of opinion respecting Guthlac B is quite harmonious in favor of the Cynewulfian authorship. That the poem consists of two distinct parts no scholar denies. Charitius³)

---

¹) Cf. Glöde, Untersuchung über die Quelle von Cynewulfs's Elene. Anglia Bd. 9, 271 ff.
²) Ten Brink's English Literature I, 55. H. M. Kennedy's translation.
³) Anglia Bd. II, S. 265—308.

following the suggestion of Rieger¹) after a penetrating investigation of the subject first concluded that Guthlac A (i. e. l. 1—790) was written by a different poet from Guthlac B (i. e. l. 791—end, and asserted that the style and manner of treatment in B points to Cynewulf. Lefévre²) after a new investigation of the whole question comes to another conclusion, making both parts³) the work of one poet and affirms that Cynewulf was that poet, but that a long period elapsed between the time of composition of A and B. Ten Brink, in the Appendix to his History of English Literature, which was written after the appearance of Charitius' article and before that of Lefévre, confesses that "he has had no leisure to enter upon the details of the question" but leans to the opinion that it is possible, nay probable, that this part (A) too was written by Cynewulf and then adds "although I admit that a new inquiry into the question would be desirable"⁴). Perhaps Wülker's opinion may be added here as a concise form of conclusion to the foregoing conflicting views as well as a statement of the present position of the critical question: 'Man darf also wohl nach wie vor auf der Meinung bestehen, auch wenn man zugiebt, dass Charitius' Abhandlung nicht in jeder Beziehung abschliessend ist, dass Guthlac v. 1—790 nicht vom selben Dichter wie v. 790—Schluss sein kann, dass aber v. 791—Schluss sehr wohl Cynewulf zugeschrieben werden darf und es sehr wohl möglich ist, dass der Dichter gegen Schluss des Werkes (der uns leider verloren ist) seinen Namen wie in anderen Gedichten, in Runen genannt habe'⁵).

The work in the following pages, so far as it relates to Elene and the Fata Apostolorum is based upon the Anglosaxon Text as found in Wülker's Bibliothek der Angelsächischen Poesie, Bd. II., 1. Hälfte, S. 126—201; and S. 87—91. For the Christ, Juliana and Guthlac B, the text as found in Grein's Bibliothek

---

[1] Zeitschrift für Deutsche Philologie, I, S. 326 Anm.
[2] Anglia Bd. VI, S. 181—240.
[3] Lefévre divides the poem into three parts of which I and II correspond to Guthlac A (l. 1—790).
[4] Ten Brink's Hist. of Engl. Lit., Vol. I, App. p. 388. H. M. Kennedy's translation.
[5] Wülker's Grundriss zur Gesch. d. Angelsächsichen Literatur, S. 183.

der Angelsächischen Poesie has been used, and the citations in the Essay are according to lines in these texts.

I purposely omit a discussion of the Judgment Day which is so graphically described in the third part of Christ and to which there are allusions in both Juliana and Elene, as I am unable to add anything to what has been already presented by Deering in his masterly and exhaustive dissertation, The Anglosaxon Poets on the Judgment Day, Leipzig, 1890.

As to the most satisfactory and correctest arrangement of the material found relevant to our theme there may be naturally difference of opinion. In preference to a greater number of chief divisions of the essay, I have chosen to make but four chief groups viz. I. Mythology, II. Religious Conceptions, III. The State and IV. Nature, and to arrange the material — which seems to me naturally thus to arrange itself — in groups according to its peculiar phase under these headings.

I. MYTHOLOGY.

That a christian Anglosaxon poet of the last half of the eighth century should show traces in his writings of the old mythology which was common to the peoples of Teutonic stock is a fact less surprising perhaps than interesting, as we must assume that the poet naturally attempted in his writings to avoid those references and allusions which would suggest to the minds of his hearers any other system of religion or worship than that which was the inspiration of his song. The traces of mythology which we find in Cynewulf's poetry are exceedingly meager and we may presume that they crept into the composition either through ignorance on the poet's part of their original significance or through adherence to set forms of expression or through conscious effort on his part to place some mythological being in unfavorable light in comparison with God.

A good example of a word which bears the stamps of mythology but which was already so removed from its original significance as to have been used probably by the poet with no thought of an earlier import is *meotud:* an original meaning of the word was probably measurer[1] and alluded to Woden a god of ways and boundaries.[2] The word is used frequently by Cynewulf but nowhere with that earlier significance which Vilmar[3] has noted in v. 128 of the Old-Saxon Heliand.

A more evident mythological allusion is the following:

---
[1] Grimm, Deutsche Mythologie, S. 20. Zweite Ausgabe. Göttingen 1844.
[2] J. M. Kemble, Saxons in England, I, 343 ff.
[3] Vilmar, Deutsche Alterthümer im Heliand, S. 8.

>   eala earendel   engla beorhtast
>   ofer middangeard   monnum sended
>   and soðfæsta   sunnan leoma
>   torht ofer tunglas!

The poet uses these words at the beginning of a lyrical outburst of praise: *earendel* is clearly used in addressing Christ. The substance of the myth as it is found in the Edda whence the name *earendel* arises is thus related: eben ist Troa geschäftig ihren Zauber auszusprechen, als zum Lohn für die nahende heilung ihr Thorr die frohe kunde bringen will dass er aus dem Norden von Iötunheim kommend im Korb auf dem Rücken ihren Mann den kühnen Örvandil getragen habe, der nun bald heimkehren müsse: zum Wahrzeichen fügt er hinzu Orvandils zehe sei aus dem Korb vorgestanden und erfroren weshalb er sie abgebrochen und an den Himmel geworfen und daraus einen Stern erschaffen habe der Örvandilsta heisst.[1]) Perhaps this is as much of the fable as concerns us here, as the chief point of interest is the fact that Örvandilsta the name given to this star thus wonderfully created belongs to a mythological saga[2]) and that cognate with it is *earendel* by which Christ is addressed.[3])

Allusions to *Wyrd*, a controller of human destiny, are extremely sparse in the Cynewulfian poems. The word *wyrd* occurs but once in all Crist (v. 81) and is used then in its most abstract sense. Perhaps twice in Cynewulf its use recalls the goddess whose decrees ruled human destiny.[4])

>   wyrd ne meahte
>   in fægum leng   feorg gehealden
>   deore fraetwe   þonne him gedemed wæs.
>   (G. v. 1030 ff.)

[1]) Grimm's Deutsche Mythologie. S. 346.
[2]) Cf. for the Orendelsaga, also B. Symons in Paul's Grundriss der Germanischen Philologie, Bd. 2, Abtheilung 1, S. 62, and Mogk, in Paul's Grundriss I, S. 1095.
[3]) Grimm, Mythologie. S 348, "auf den Namen bezieht sich ohne Zweifel, dass in Ags. glossen earendel jubar ausdrückt".
[4]) "Aus allen stellen des germanischen Alterthums, wo Uröd auftritt, geht hervor, dass es einst in der Vorstellung unserer Vorfahren eine Macht gegeben haben muss, in deren Gewalt sich der Germane das Geschick der Menschen dachte." Mogk in Paul's Grundriss, I, S. 1024.

We may assume here that the christian poet purposely refers to *wyrd* as being unable to do something, or rather to prevent something from happening which has been decreed by another and higher tribunal thus bringing into unfavourable comparison the being whose decrees were believed to rule gods as well as men. We have also one clear reference to a decree of Fate in the Cynewulfian poetry, and only one:

huru Wyrd ȝescreaf
þæt he swa ȝeleafful and swa leof ȝode
in worldrice weorðan sceolde
Criste ȝecweme: (E. v. 1046 ff.)

Wyrd decreed that he (Judas) should become so faithful etc. It is undoubtedly a direct allusion to the mythological *Wyrd*. *Wefen wyrdstafum* (G. v. 1325) recalls the spinning of the Parcae. There is nothing remarkable about the use of the word in Juliana (v. 33, 538). The two references cited above to the *wyrd* of mythology are the only ones in the forty-four hundred lines of poetry ascribed to Cynewulf. As compared with Beowulf where eight or nine such uses occur in less than thirty two hundred lines, the Cynewulfian forms are comparatively free from this mark of heathenism, a fact which does not accord with Kemble's remark respecting the conception and use of *wyrd* that: „in this respect there is no difference whatever between the practice in Beowulf and the more professedly christian poems of the Exeter and Vercelli codices, or Cædmon." [1]

Several formulas recalling *wyrd* may be pointed out: *swylt calle fornam* (J. v. 675) is the description of the destruction of Helisens and his followers: *sume wiȝ fornam* (E. v. 131): *sume drenc fornam* (E. v. 136), *or þec swylt nime* (E. v. 447, J. v. 255); *deað in ȝeðronȝ* (G. v. 835): *deað nealæcte, slop stilȝonȝum . . . . sohte sawelhus* (G. v. 1112 f.) (cf. also C v. 1603, J. v. 255) suggest a belief in Fate, and are varieties of impersonations of death.

The old work of giants *eald enta ȝeweorc* (Beow. 2775) and *enta ȝeweorc* (Beow. 2718), *enta ærȝeweorc* (Beow. 1680) of Beowulf finds but one example that approaches a parallel in the Cynewulfian poems, *burȝentu* (E. v. 31). Just what this word refers

---

[1] Kemble, S. in E. I, p. 401.

to is difficult to say, but as popular belief peopled England with giants in prehistoric times, we are perhaps justified in assuming that the reference here is to some old structure, castle or wall whose origin was unknown.

The Anglosaxon christian attributed to paradise, the condition of sinless bliss to which he looked back in distinction with the heaven to which he looked forward, a set of qualities suitable to a golden age. It was the Garden of Eden, the *neorxna wong*, the plain resplendent with riches and brilliant with hues (C. v. 1392), a glorious dwelling (J. v. 503), where was neither waning of riches nor loss of life, nor disease of body, nor cessation of conviviality, nor coming of death, but one might, without any sin's pollution, live in that home, long revelling in renewed joys, and after a certain period *fyrst* might betake himself body, limbs and spirit together to the everlasting joys of the kingdom of heaven (G. v. 800 ff.) where he should enjoy the light of the Lord's countenance.

There are other words and allusions, as we shall see further on when we come to speak of the conception of the 'devil' and of 'hell', which are decidedly heathen and have a mythological background: but they are such as are so interwoven with christian conceptions that I deem it advisable to speak of them in connection with the christian setting in which they are found. I pass therefore to consider in the next section the religious conceptions presented in the poems.

II. RELIGIOUS CONCEPTIONS.

We are employed with the most professedly christian poems of the Anglosaxon literature. They bear testimony in nearly every line to the christian zeal and enthusiasm of their author. The diction and form of expression are teeming with evidence of the deepest religious fervour but at the same time they are intertwined with a rich legacy of epic expression, and conceptions common to the Anglosaxon heroic poems. They bear all the marks of being — as they are in fact — the expression of a people buoyant in adherence to the principles of a new faith, from whose mind however the memory and constraining influences of the cults to which they had become apostate had not as yet disappeared entirely. The poems betray these characteristics not only as regards their author but also in respect to the purpose for which they were composed. They are adapted to a people prone to apostasy. The endless variation and repetition, the concrete setting of abstract themes, the recurrence of warning and admonition are all evidence of this. I purpose in the following sections to examine these christian conceptions, and to note how and to what extent they were moulded by older beliefs or influenced through effort on the poet's part to put truths, necessarily abstract, in a more comprehensive and concrete form.

1. GOD AND CHRIST.

It is granted that God and Christ are not equivalent terms. There are instances where it is evident that the writer had in mind God the Father e. g. C. v. 355 *ecan frean* and here it is shown only by the context. There are too many instances where the reference is clearly to Christ: but apart from those instances where the text or context clearly shows of which the poet is speaking occur a great number of appellations of the Deity where it is absolutely impossible to tell which is meant. In general the usage warrants us in saying that all the attributes of the Father except of course his Fatherhood are ascribable to the Son and all the attributes of the Son except his sonship to the Father and the distinguishing characteristics of the one or the other in the text or context are the simple terms Father and Son, some allusion to fatherhood or sonship or reference to the Divine Life on earth. Otherwise they are treated as one Being with two equal personalities. It has therefore seemed best to me to speak of both together.

The Anglosaxon fondness for synonyms, circumlocutions, variations and descriptive names is nowhere else so manifest in the poems as in the names given to the christian Deity. Mr. Gollancz' vocabulary[1]) to his edition of Crist contains about eighteenhundred and seventy words: there are about eighty of these, or more than four per cent, used directly as appellations of Christ and God. Elene and Fata Apostolorum are also rich in this respect — more so than Juliana and Guthlac. I know of no better way to present the various and manifold conceptions of the Divinity than by a presentation of them, along with their descriptive and qualifying adjectives, in the order of their frequency.

Most often we meet the word *god* which may designate either Father or Son. The Deity is the God of spirits *gasta god* (C. v. 130), of hosts *weoroda* (C. v. 407, 631, J. v. 515, E. v. 1149), of the powers of heaven *heofon mæʒna* (C. v. 1218, *mæʒena* (E. v. 809), of heaven's angels *heofonenʒla* (C. v. 642), of the heavenly kingdom *heofonrices* (J. v. 239, E. v. 1124), of glory *wuldres* (J. v. 180, G. v. 1051), of origins *frumða* (E. v. 345, 502), of all glories *ealra þrymma* (E. v. 519), of victory *siʒora* (E. v. 1307). Further he is a living *lifʒende* (C. v. 273, 755), saving *nerʒende* (C. v. 364), mighty *meahtiʒ* (C. v. 686, 1008), all-ruling *alwealda* (C. v. 1191), eternal *ecne* (J. v. 134), true *soðne* (J. v. 17) and holy *haliʒ* (E. v. 679) God.

[1] Prof. Cook in Modern Language Notes of America, Vol. 8, p. 54, has shown that several words have been inadvertently omitted from this list.

The conception of God as king was a favorite idea and the manifold attributes which were ascribed to the Deity in this relation may be seen from the following: King of heaven *heofones cyning* (C. v. 61, E. v. 170, 367 etc.) *ealra cyninga cyning* (C. v. 136, 215, J. v. 289), *haeleða cyning* (C. v. 372), *heahengla cyning* (C. v. 528), *wuldres cyning* (C. v. 565, J. v. 516, F. A. v. 27), *elmura gehwaes cyning* (C. v. 703), *alwihta cyning* (C. v. 687), *cyning anboren* (C. v. 618, E. v. 392), *wuldorcyning* (E. v. 291, F. A. v. 74), *radorcyning* (E. v. 624, C. v. 727, J. v. 447), *cyning æhmihtig* (E. v. 865, G. v. 794), *tirmeahtig cyning* (C. v. 1166), *æðelcyning* (C. v. 904), *heahcyning* (C. v. 150), *se mihtiga cyning* (E. v. 941), *soð cyning* (E. v. 444, J. v. 224), *riht cyning* (C. v. 181), *prymcyning* (E. v. 494), *morgencyning* C. v. 917, E. v. 1247), *weoroda wuldorcyning* (C. v. 161), *gesceafta scircyning* (C. v. 1153), *sigora soðcyning* (C. v. 1229).

Scarcely less often is the christian Divinity referred to as *frea* and the following are variations of the conception which this word, which probably meant to Cynewulf nothing else than Lord, yields, Lord of victories *sigora frean* (J. v. 361, G. v. 1053), of angels (E. v. 1306), almighty Lord *frea ælmihtig* (C. v. 395), mighty Lord *frea mihtig* (C. v. 475, E. v. 680, 1067), exalted Lord of heaven *heofona heah-frea* (C. v. 253, 424), true Lord of victory *soð sigores frea* (C. v. 404, E. v. 488) and Lord of all creation *frean ealra gesceafta* (C. v. 925 f.).

One of the commonest words to designate the Deity is *dryhten*, Lord, Sovereign. As a simple word it refers invariably to the Deity, as a compound word it may refer to earthly rulers, (cf. G. v. 984, 1124 etc). That the word has any special reference to God as commander or general, as Kent remarks[1], I am unable to see. An examination of the twenty-two uses of the word in Crist or of its use in Guthlac or Elene itself will not, in my opinion, sustain this view. It is generally used unqualified to denote God as a careful examination of its uses shows, and although the expressions *god dryhten* (E. v. 759) and *dryhten hælend* (E. v. 725) do occur, they are, in comparison with the scores of uses without such appositives, scanty ground from which

---

[1] Kent, Teutonic Antiquities in Andreas and Elene, pag. 11.

to infer that "this would seem to indicate a sort of necessity for designating more exactly the christian significance of the word". (Kent. p. 11.). We find this variation of the thought in connection with *dryhten:* everlasting *ece* (C. v. 272, 366, 396, 711 etc.), true *soð* (C. v. 512), and mighty *meahtiȝ* (C. v. 868) Lord: the Lord of heaven *heofona* (C. v. 348), of lords *dryhtna* (C. v. 405), of hosts *weoroda* (C. v. 428, E. v. 896), *duȝuða* (C. v. 782, E. v. 81), of victory *siȝora* (E. v. 346) and of all mankind *ealra hæleða cynnes* (E. v. 187 f.).

The Divinity is thought of not only as king, invested with pomp and majesty, but also as a monarch exercising the authority invested in him, as a Ruler *waldend:* the One at whose control are events *wyrda* (E. v. 80): the Ruler of angels *engla* (C. v. 474), of heaven (C. v. 755), of powers *meahta* (C. v. 823, J. v. 723), *mihta* (E. v. 337), of the skies *rodera* (C. v. 866, J. v. 305, E. v. 206), of men *weoroda* (C. v. 1570, E. v. 788), *þeoda* (E. v. 421), *mæȝena* (E. v. 347), of victory *siȝora* (E. v. 731): in short the Ruler of all *ealles waldend* (C. v. 577, E. v. 512).

The Lord is too, often called *meotud*, thus *meotud moncynnes* (C. v. 244, J. v. 182, 436), *mæȝen-cyningȝa* (C. v. 943). In connection with the creation the word seems to mean Creator in (C. v. 14, 1380, E. v. 726).

Christ is viewed from the standpoint of the various attributes of his character, and aspects of his mission, thus rescuing Christ *crist nerȝende* (C. v. 157), almighty Christ *crist ælmihtig* (C. v. 215, 331), saving Christ *hælende crist* (C. v. 250), Saviour Christ *hælend crist* (C. v. 358) and finally the crucified Christ *þone ahanȝnan crist* (E. v. 797). It is singular that this word which has given its name to the longest of the Cynewulfian poems is not found once in the second part of the same, neither is it found in Guthlac B, although occurring quite frequently in the other divisions of these poems and in Juliana and Elene.

As an offspring of God, Christ is the Son *sunu* (C. v. 94, 143, 197, 210, 451 etc.), *soð sunu meotudes* (E. v. 461, 474, 564 etc.), of the Father *fæder* (C. v. 110), of man *monnes* (C. v. 126). He is, further, the bright *beorhtne* (C. v. 205), the dear *se deora* (J. v. 725) and the sinless *synna leas* (E. v. 777) Son. The Son

co-dwelling with thy only Lord *efencardiʒende mid þinne enʒan
frean* (C. v. 237), the one-born Son *ancenned sunu* (C. v. 464).
of the Lord *dryhtnes* (C. v. 297), of the Ruler *waldendes* (C. v. 635).
God's spirit Son *ʒodes ʒæstsunu* (C. v. 660, E. v. 673).

He is also the *bearn*, one born, child. This relation to God
is emphatically expressed in three instances by a coordinate placing
of *bearn* and *sunu*, thus: *mihtig meotudes bearn* and *se monnes
sunu* (C. v. 126); *beorhtne sunu bearn eacen ʒodes* (C. v. 205);
ancenned sunu, efenece bearn aʒnum fæder (C. v. 464 f.). He
is also *ʒodes aʒen bearn* (C. v. 572, E. v. 179, 422 etc.) *ʒodes
ece bearn* C. v. 744. *þæt æðele bearn* (C. v. 1195); *æðelust bearna*
(E. v. 476), *siʒebearn ʒodes* (E. v. 481, 862, 1146); *ealra siʒebearna
þæt seleste and æðeleste* (C. v. 520 f.). *bearn waldendes* (E. v. 391,
J. v. 266), *freobearn* (C. v. 224, E. v. 672), *frumbearn* (C. v. 507),
ʒælbearn (C. v. 499, E. v. 719) and *hælubearn* (C. v. 586, 754).

Þeoden, prince, sovereign, king often designates the Deity
(C. v. 541, 553, G. v. 1230, E. v. 487, 776, etc.). God is the
King of angels *enʒla þeoden* (C. v. 332, E. v. 857), and the glorious
Prince *þeoden þrymfæst* C. v. 457, 944). As God was often
designated as king and ruler so he is likewise often viewed as
Creator, *scyppend*. He is the mild *milde* (C. v. 417) and radiant
scinende (C. v. 1220) Creator of men *hæleða* (C. v. 266), of powers
mihta (G. v. 1131), of spirits *ʒæsta* (J. v. 18) *ʒasta* (E. v. 790);
and finally the bright Creator of all *þone sciran scyppend ealra*
E. v. 370). As the Anglosaxon king was the guardian of his
people and realm so the Deity is the guardian of angels *enʒla
weard* (E. v. 1315) and of the heavenly kingdom *heofonrices*
(J. v. 212), of the skies *rodera* (C. v. 134), of spirits *ʒasta* (E. v.
1021), of life *lifes* (C. v. 1613), of heaven *wuldres* (E. v. 84), of
victory *siʒores* (C. v. 243), *siʒora* (C. v. 1517), and of the folk
folces (C. v. 1648), *folca* C. (v. 946).

Eðelinʒ, the one of noble origin, prince lord, applies to
Christ. He is heaven's Prince *wuldres æðelinʒ* (C. v. 158). The
expression *æðelinʒa ord* (C. v. 515, E. v. 393) exalts Christ by
making Him the chief of princes. He is also the *fruma*, the
Prince, the Source, of life *lifes* (C. v. 44, E. v. 792), *liffruma*
(C. v. 504, 656 etc.), of hosts *herʒa* (C. v. 845, E. v. 210). A stronger ex-

pression is *ordfruma* (E. A. 28) although almost tautological in itself: the noble Founder *æðelne ordfruman* (C. v. 402), the Source of blessing *eades ordfruma* (C. v. 1199); *ece eadfruma* (C. v. 532) the bright Prince of glory *torhtes tirfruma(n)* (C. v. 206) and the Prince of all peoples *ealra folca fruma* (C. v. 516).

Viewing the Divinity in the aspect of a Protector who shields his own as the helmet shields the head of the wearer He is the *Helm* of men *wera* (E. v. 475), of spirits (E. v. 176), of the holy ones *haligra* (C. v. 529), of heaven (J. v. 722), of the heavenly kingdom (C. v. 556) and of all creatures *alwihta* (C. v. 274, 410). *Agend* views the Divinity in still another light: He is the possessor of victory *sigores agend* (C. v. 420), and of life *lifes* (C. v. 471), of heaven *swegles* (C. v. 543), and of glory (J. v. 223, C. v. 1198). A relatively common appellation is *hlaford* Lord (C. v. 461, 498, 518, E. v. 175). As judge also *dema* is Christ represented and especially in connection with the Last Judgment. It is singular that the line *fore onsyne eces deman* occurs four times in the poems we are studying (C. v. 796, 836; G. v. 1161; E. v. 745), (cf. also G. v. 755). *Nergend*, Savior, of peoples *folca* (C. v. 426), of souls *sawla* (C. v. 571, E. v. 461, 798), of men *fira* (J. v. 240, E. v. 1077, 1172), *niða* (E. v. 503, 1085).

A function of the Anglosaxon king was the giving of presents and the bestowing of gifts upon certain occasions and for certain services (cf. Judith v. 30, 93 and Beo. v. 1488), and in this capacity he was the *brytta*, the distributor: doubtless in allusion to this custom of the early Teutonic monarch is it that the title of *brytta* is given to God. He is the *lifes brytta* (C. v. 334) and the *swegles brytta* (C. v. 281) and *tires brytta* (C. v. 462). The same word applies to Constantine (E. v. 194). *Brego* used as well of heathen princes as of the christian Deity cf. Judith v. 39) occurs twice only *halig heahengu brego* (C. v. 103), and *se brego(o) mæra* (C. v. 156). *Beorn*, the hero, the warrior designates Christ in only two instances (C. v. 419, 530). The same word applies to the warriors often in Elene; it also designates those who shall be distressed at the coming of Christ C. v. 992). Christ as the Savior is often expressed by *se hælend*

(C. v. 383, 505, E. v. 861, 911 etc). He is also the hallowed One *se ʒehalʒoda* (C. v. 435).

There are numerous other appellations which are used but once or twice: some clearly biblical in origin, some as clearly taken from surrounding life and relations: we find still the following variety: *ealdor* (C. v. 8), *reccend* (C. v. 18), *siʒedryhten* (C. v. 128), *eces alwaldan* (C. v. 140), *sineʒiefa* (C. v. 460), *wilʒiefa* (C. v. 537, E. v. 814), *hæleða hyhtʒiefa* (E. v. 851), *weoroda wuldorʒiefa* (E. v. 681), *eorla eadʒiefa* (C. v. 546): *feorhʒiefa* (C. v. 556): *wiʒendra hleo* (C. v. 409): *ʒæsta hleo* (J. v. 49): *beorna hleo* (J. v. 272): *mæʒna ʒoldhord* (C. v. 787): *ryhtend* (C. v. 798): *weallstan* (C. v. 2): *se cræftiʒa* (C. v. 12): *earendel* (C. v. 104) (cf. p. 6): *soðfæstra sunnan leoma* (C. v. 106): *soðfæstra leoht* (E. v. 7): *word ʒodes* (C. v. 120): *emmanuhel* (C. v. 132): þone *clænan sacerd* (C. v. 136 f.): *æbrinʒende* (C. v. 140): *ʒæsta ʒeocend* (G. v. 1106, C. v. 198, E. v. 682): *lifes* þrym (C. v. 204): *ealra* þrymma þrym (E. v. 483, C. v. 726): *ealles leohtes leoht* (E. v. 486); *albru cyninʒa* þrym (E. v. 815): *wuldres* þrym (J. v. 641); *rodera* þrym (C. v. 423): *beorna wuldor* (E. v. 186): *cyninʒa wuldor* (C. v. 508): þrymmes hyrde (J. v. 280, E. v. 348, 858): þæs *lareowes* (C. v. 458): *lifes lattio* (E. v. 520); *se earenanstan* (C. v. 1196): *sellend siʒora* (J. v. 668): *mildne mundboran* (J. v. 213): *wiʒena wyn* (J. v. 641); *dæda demend* (J. v. 725): *se ælmihtiʒ* (G. v. 923); *fæder enʒla* (E. v. 783): *fæder moneynnes* (F. A 29) and *fæder ælmihtiʒ* (E. v. 1083).

We have thus noticed more than one hundred and fifty different expressions, many of them very similar in thought and differentiating from each other often by very slight shades of meaning. Many of them doubtless as *wiʒendra hleo*, *sineʒiefa*, *tires brytta*, *rices weard*, *helm wera* were terms customarily applied to the rulers and leaders of the Anglosaxons themselves and recall the qualities and attributes of the overlord of the people who must be their protector (E. v. 99) and the guardian of his own realm. The monarch was also the dispenser of glory the *tires brytta*, to those whose services were distinguished by particular merit. The Anglosaxon poet was fond of almost endless variation in his terminology and this doubtless accounts for many of the

2

noted expressions, but besides this inclination which is noticeable everywhere in Anglosaxon poetry, the poet is here striving to make a necessarily abstract theme as concrete as possible; and so presents to his hearers, to whom the idea of the Godhead must be still more obscure and abstract than to himself, the conception of the christian Deity in terms of the loftiest conception of a human being with which he or they were familiar i. e. presents the Deity often in the guise of their own rulers, and ascribes to him the attributes and functions of an earthly king.

The great majority of these expressions embody conceptions peculiar to the Anglosaxon. The only expressions whence the foregoing could have been taken, used in the Latin homilies which have served as a source of Crist and in the hymn Apparebi repentina dies etc. (if we accept it as a source of the third part of Crist) and in the selections from the Acta Sanctorum upon which Juliana, Guthlac and Elene[1]) are based are: dominus noster, dominus deus, deus homo, redemptor noster, Jesus Christus, deus pater, judex, judex altus, magnus judex, justus arbiter, gloriosus rex, deus caeli et terrae, vitae dator, solus verus deus, unus deus omnipotens, creator omnium saeculorum, unus potens, deus benedictus in saecula, pater, filius, Salvator noster, Filius dei.

The multiformity of expression in the Anglosaxon as compared with the Latin is strikingly large; it betokens the poet's veneration for and devotion to the Source of the belief which is extolled in his song; and this very reverence, coupled with motives of a didactic character, aided, we may assume, in carrying him to an amplitude of conception which was not satisfied to clothe itself in biblical and ecclesiastical phraseology, but takes on as well the mode of expression of the heroic poems with which he was possibly acquainted[2]).

2. THE HOLY SPIRIT AND THE TRINITY.

I treat these two subjects together because of the scarcity of references to them and because we can conceive of the Holy

[1]) Cf. Glöde, Anglia, Bd. IX, S. 271 ff. Ueber die Quelle von Cynewulf's Elene.
[2]) Cf. Sarrazin in Anglia Bd. IX, S. 515 ff. Ueber Beowulf und Kynewulf.

Spirit as mentioned in a few instances only when we recognize it as constituting one of the elements of the Trinity. The Holy Spirit is alluded to much less often than the other members of the Godhead; yet in several instances the references are distinct. I do not understand that a third member of the Godhead is meant wherever we meet the word ȝæst but think that this word is often used metonymically for the Godhead (cf. C. v. 207, J. v. 724, E. v. 1105). By the Spirit of heaven sweȝles ȝæst (C. v. 203) we are in doubt as to whether the Holy Spirit as a distinct agent is meant. The reference is certainly to a distinct agent also in Crist v. 709 ff. where we are told that the welfare of the disciples continued, after their Lord's ascension, through the spirit's grace

þurh ȝæstes ȝiefe   ȝodes þeȝna blæd
æfter upstiȝe   ecan dryhtnes.

hwæðre forð biewom

Juliana's constant companion was the Holy Spirit hyre wæs haliȝ ȝæst sinȝal ȝesið (J. v. 241 f.). The expression bærn inc is ȝemæne heahȝæst hleofæst (C. v. 357 f.) is plainly a recognition of the third member of the Godhead. In C. v. 774, the Spirit is made cordinate with the Son of God. biddan bearn ȝodes and þone bliðan ȝæst. The Holy Spirit shall lock the fiends in hell (C. v. 1624); (Cf. also Andreas v. 1002 þurh handhrine haliȝes ȝæstes). The Holy Ghost was imparted to Judas him wæs haliȝ ȝæst befolen (E. v. 935); it makes its abode in Helen's heart ond þa wic beheold haliȝ heofonlic ȝæst (E. v. 1143 f.). Numerous allusions to the gift of the spirit ȝæstes ȝiefe (E. v. 199, 1057, 1156) would seem to indicate merely a special manifestation of Divine Power. The above references indicate that the Holy Spirit was viewed in different lights, that it was personified (J. v. 241 f. C. v. 1624), that it was viewed merely as a means or agent (C. v. 709 f., J. v. 724 f.) and last, it was a specific manifestation or emanation from God (E. v. 199, 1067). These and the following references to the Trinity leave no doubt as to the fact of the recognition of the three members of the Godhead, though as occupying different degrees of importance perhaps; for the attributes of the Father and Son which were seen to be very similar are very sparingly ascribed to the Holy Spirit.

The Trinity is seldom mentioned. It is once addressed

ea la seo wlitiȝe   weorðmynda full
heah and haliȝ   heofoncund þrynis   (C. v. 378 f.)

It is invested with honor and glory, exaltation and holiness, and further, to it are ascribed everlasting thanks:

wuldor þæs aȝe
þrynesse þrym   þone butan ende   (C. v. 598 f.)

In Elene there is one allusion and it is of little interest:

hu se ȝasta helm
in þrynesse   þrymme ȝeweorðad
acenned weard.   (E. v. 176 f.)

In Juliana the Trinity is represented as sitting in Judgment at the Last Day and ascribing to men reward according to their works, þonne seo þrynis þrymsittende in annesse ælda cynne etc. (J. v. 724 f.). These are all of the references to the Trinity. They are enough to show clearly that three members of the Godhead were recognized and that they were thought of as acting independently and alone and also in unison as One.

3. VIRGIN MARY.

Crist alone of the poems presents traces of Mariolatry. These traces too are of the most pronounced character. The virgin is extolled as the young woman *seo fæmne ȝeong* (C. v. 35), the maid without blemish *mæȝð mænes leas* (C. v. 36) and the purest woman on earth of those who have lived through all ages

seo cleneste   ewen ofer eorðan
þara þe ȝewurde   to widan feore   (C. v. 276 f.).

She is glorified as the joy of women throughout the hosts of glory and the noblest maid o'er all the expanse of earth

wifa wynn   ȝeond wuldres þrym
fæmne freolicast   ofer ealne folde sceat   (C. v. 71 f.)

She is recognised in heaven upon earth and in hell, for all those upon earth endowed with speech call her the bride *bryd* of the most excellent Ruler of heaven *þæs selestan sweȝles bryttan* (C. v. 278 f.); and likewise the most exalted thanes of Christ in heaven speak and sing of her as endowed with holy virtues, the queen of the hosts of glory, of the races of the world under heaven and of the inhabitants of hell,

> þæt þu sie hlæfdige halgum meahtum
> wuldorweorudes and worldcundra
> hada under heofonum and helwara! (C. v. 284 f.).

She is the recipient of worship and the answerer of prayer: the city-dwellers pray to her to make known the Comfort, her own Son, to the folk:

> huru þæs biddað burgsittende
> þæt þu þa frofre folcum cyðe
> þinre sylfre sunu. (C. v. 337.)

She is further represented as an intercessor. The inhabitants of the world are represented as requesting her to plead their cause for them that the Son may not leave them longer in this vale of death to follow error but that he may conduct them into the kingdom of the Father.

> Geðinga us nu þristum wordum
> þæt he us ne læte leng owihte
> in þisse deaðdene gedwolan hyran
> ac þæt he usic geferge in fæder rice. (C. v. 342 f.).

4. HEAVEN.

Analogous to the foregoing concrete conception of the Deity we find in many instances that the Anglosaxon's conception of heaven was adapted to his way of thinking of governmental institutions and national customs. Consistent with the conception of the Deity as clothed with the prerogatives of an earthly ruler, is the representation of heaven, his dwelling place, (C. v. 103, 506 etc.) as a kingdom *rice* (C. v. 353), the choicest of royal dominions *cynestola cyst* (C. v. 51), the hereditary abode of Christ *eðel* (C. v. 741), the bright dwelling places *beorhtra bolda* (C. v. 742) and the citadel of Christ *cristes burglond* (C. v. 51), the bright city *in þære beorhtan byrig* (E. v. 821), the eternal possessions *ecra gestealda* (E. v. 801). The representation of heaven as a citadel or city or as a bright abode is again a peculiarly graphic putting of an idea perhaps ill-defined but which the poet wishes to make comprehensible to his hearers: to do this he indulges in his customary variation of the phraseology, designating it further as the hereditary abode of angels *enzla edel* (C. v. 630) and the long home *langue ham* (F. A. 92) thus appealing to the instinctive love of family life and the value attached to personal possessions.

The adaptation of the theme to the Anglosaxon's way of thinking becomes more evident upon a consideration of the characteristics of heaven, of what its joys are and how its inhabitants spend their time. Distinct reminiscences of Anglosaxon customs are here carried over into his portrayal of heaven's joys. To obtain almost a complete picture of all that the zealous Anglosaxon mind pictured to itself as awaiting the righteous soul in heaven perhaps we need to do little more than read carefully (C. v. 1640—1665).

Before everything else the *dream* constituted one of the joys of heaven. In every essay of the character of this I believe that the discussion of the word by Grimm (Vorrede to Andreas and Elene, S. XXXVII) has been accepted as satisfactory. It is referred to the joy and mirth of drinking companions as, free from care, they sat together in the merry circle of the mead-hall. This pleasure being perhaps the acme of all joys, according to the early Teuton's conception, was the more readily transferred to his conception of heaven which he termed the *dream unhwilen* (E. v. 1231) and the *sindream* (G. v. 811) and the *dream after deade* (F. A. v. 81), the true joy *þone soðan gefean* (F. A. v. 80). The expression is intensified where Crist is said to conduct his folk into the joy of joys *in dreama dream* (C. v. 580). The loss of this joyous association is emphasized in the paraphrase of Matt. 25:41 where Christ sentences the condemned to depart into everlasting fire: the poet not satisfied with the plain expression of the Vulgate inserts an idea of his own — of their own choice deprived of the joys of angels — *willum bescyrede enzla dreames* (C. v. 1520 f.).

This *dream* is in the nature of a reward too: it is the reward of victory *sizelean* (F. A. v. 81) which the victorious warrior receives after the tumult of battles and the fierce war-play (F. A. v. 20 — a reward of victory *sizores to leane* (F. A. v. 61) which was in store in the glorious dwelling *beorhtne boldwelan*

(F. A. v. 31), and granted by the lord of the dwelling as meed of battle *wiʒʒes lean* (E. v. 824, F. A. v. 74), *selust siʒeleuna seald in heofonum* (E. v. 527). Many other instances might be cited to show that heaven was thought of often as a guerdon for valor and victory in fight, that as a gracious and beneficent sovereign granted rewards and honors and life of peace to his faithful followers, so heaven is the place where the same blessings in a greater degree and for a longer time are granted by a greater Sovereign as reward for victorious and faithful life. It is hardly necessary to call attention to the similarity of this conception to the old Scandinavian conception of Walhalla the blessed abode for which the brave warrior longed and whither he expected to be conducted in case of death on the battlefield, there in company with brave comrades to be a child of Woden and participate in the various jovialities of the abode of joy.

The characteristics of heaven are enumerated most fully in Crist v. 1640 ff. a passage which, though interesting in itself, contains little that is not strictly biblical. The conception that locates the abode of Christ in the East could well have been suggested by Matth. 24:27, but as this is not the usual teaching of the Bible, I take it, that the frequent reference to heaven as located in the East is due to some existing tradition or belief which has been brought into the service of the christian worship. We are told that preceding the Lord as he comes to Judgment shall come a ray of the sun from the Southeast *suðan eastan sunnan leoma cymeð* (C. v. 901 f.): then the Child of God shall appear through the gates of heaven *þurh heofona ʒehleodu hider oðywed* (C. v. 905): then the countenance of Christ shall come gloriously, the radiance of the noble king from the East of heaven

   cymeð wunderlic Cristes onsyn
   æðeleyninʒes wlite eastan from roderum (C. v. 906 f.).

This corresponds to the narrative in the Genesis where God's abode is located in the South and East *þæt is suð and east* (Genesis v. 669): it is in harmony also with the custom of the christian of that time who worshipped with his face to the East and with hands lifted toward the rising sun in contradistinction with the praying heathen who faced the North during his worship. (Grimm, Mythologie, S. 30).

The perpetuity of the coveted heavenly blessedness as compared with the transient unenduring pleasures of this life worked especially forcibly upon the mind of the Anglosaxon poet and he seldom fails to allude to this aspect of heaven when opportunity is afforded. Some of his variations of the expression are *a to worulde forð* (C. v. 101), *wide ferhð* (C. v. 163), *a butan ende* (C. v. 271), *ealne widan feore* (C. v. 439), *in ecnesse* (C. v. 1204), *to widan feore* (C. v. 1344, G. v. 812), *awo* (C. v. 1664), *awo to ealdre* (C. v. 1616), *to worulde* (G. v. 786), *a,* (G. v. 1163, 811).

5. ANGELS.

The poet displays a fondness of thinking of the angels as existing and moving in collective bodies as they perform the service of the Father in heaven or go on his missions to the world. They act in multitudes or throngs as the following designations of their collective bodies show: *þreat* (G. v. 1288), *ᵹedryht* (C. v. 942), *weorud* (C. v. 493), *heap* (C. v. 554), *ᵹelac* (C. v. 896), *scolu* (C. v. 929), *here* (C. v. 930), *wöeldu.ᵹnð* (C. v. 1012), *þrym* (C. v. 1069) and *corðor* (C. v. 494).

They are often introduced individually also in the role of messengers of God. It was an angel of God that miraculously saved the holy Juliana as she was about to be cremated; it was a divine angel *enᵹel ufancunde* (G. v. 1216) that communed with Guthlac every morning and evening, imparting to him spiritual strength; likewise Gabriel the archangel of heaven *heofones heahenᵹel* (C. v. 202) was God's errand-bearer *ᵹodes spelboda*, the transmitter of the divine tidings to the Virgin; it was also a gleaming ambassador of heaven *wlitiᵹ wuldres boda* (E. v. 77) that brought the injunctions of the King of Heaven to Constantine. God promised to send his messengers *aras* (C. v. 759) to protect the righteous against the dart-showers of the evil workers. In the capacity of emissary or representative of the Heavenly King the angel is a thane *þeᵹn* (G. v. 1217), *heahboda* (C. v. 295), *spelboda* (C. v. 336), *boda* (C. v. 449), messenger of joy *wilboda* (G. v. 1220), and *ar* (C. v. 192). These words *spelboda*, *boda*, or etc., are elsewhere applied to the ambassadors of earthly kings and perhaps their use here may justify the assumption that the poet pictured to himself the angels as the honored courtiers and servants who were ever present at the court of the Monarch of Heaven, ready to do his bidding.

The angels are gleaming in appearance in signification of their holiness, exaltation and purity of character in comparison with evil spirits which are often represented as sombre or black in appearance (cf. C. v. 896 f.). The messenger to Constantine is described as *ƿlitescine* (E. v. 72) *hwit*, and *hiurbeorhte*, and as he appeared his own radiance dispelled the shadows of the night *nihthelm toglad*: and the light disappeared with the angel. Several descriptions in Crist also represent them as radiant *ƿlitescine* (C. v. 554, 493), or white *hwite* (C. v. 545) or exceedingly bright *ælbeorht* (C. v. 548, 929, 1277). The angelic messenger to Juliana was gleaming with trappings *frætwum blican* (J. v. 564) and the same words describe the appearance of the two angels which the disciples saw at the ascension of Christ (C. v. 507), though here it may well be considered a paraphrase of the expression Acts 1:10 "two men stood by in white raiment".

The multitude of the heavenly host *mægenþrym* (C. v. 352 f.) have the care of the glorious dwelling of the Prince in the kingdom of heaven — and do his offices —, a conception which suggests strongly the relation of courtiers to the monarch and to his royal abode. They are his thanes that speak and sing the praise of the Virgin, *cristes þegnas cwædud and sinᵹað* (C. v. 283). They voice songs of praise to lifes Creator (C. v. 502 f.) and their song shall constitute one of the joys of heaven (C. v. 1650). Very noticeable is the Anglosaxon coloring given to the description in C. v. 515—557 where we are told that angels robed in splendor came to meet the Prosperity-giver of earls as he returned to the sky, bands of heavenly messengers descended in the sky to meet him and thereupon followed the greatest of banquets *symbla mæst* in glory; fitting was it that thanes thus brightly clad should come to this joy in the citadel *burᵹ* of the Prince. How nearly suitable is this to what we should expect the description of the return of a monarch of Mercia or Northumbria to be, after he had led his subjects to a glorious victory over their old foes the Britons or over a rival neighbor of Teutonic blood! The thanes that remained at home would go out rejoicing to meet him as he returned bearing the spoils and trophies of victory. We can imagine them bidding him a hearty welcome to his city, his *burʒ*, as it is here represented, and afterwards celebrating his success and victories in a mighty jubilee *symbel*.

References to the angelic hierarchies also are not wanting. The faithful race of the Seraphim *soðfæste Seraphinnes cynn* (C. v. 386 f.) in a description bearing many similarities with Isa. 6: 2, 3 are represented as having the noblest office in the service of the King *habbað folʒoðu cyst mid cyninʒe*: it is granted them to guard his presence with their wings and to disport in glorious rivalry as to which may come nearest to the Lord. In E. v. 739 ff. the Cherubim and the Seraphim are mentioned. The Cherubim are furnished with six wings each and it is theirs to sing continually the praise of the heavenly King and to perform his service, over in his presence. There are two which are called Seraphim and their duty is to guard the approach to the Paradise and the tree of life, with flaming sword; they brandish the dangerous blade *hearderʒ cwacað, beofað broʒdenmæl*, are armed with genuine Anglosaxon battle armor. It is peculiar that the same offices are assigned to the Seraphim in Crist that the Cherubim are spoken of as performing in Elene. Kent (p. 20) has noted that the order in which the hierarchies are mentioned in both Andreas and Elene, if intended to indicate relative rank, is just the opposite of that usually given: for the first order of the hierarchy was Seraphim and the second Cherubim; moreover in the Genesis account (Gen. 3:24) it is the Cherubim which guard the approach to Paradise and the tree of life. It were perhaps bold to affirm that the poet confused here the two words for a moment, yet when we consider the points of similarity in the description of the Seraphim in Crist and the Cherubim in Elene, the indentity of the two seems most natural. The reference to their service of the King, their flight about him, their continual enjoyment of his presence, their radiance and their song, beginning in Crist *haliʒ eart þu halig heahengla breʒo*, and in Elene *haliʒ* is se halȝa heahengla ȝod, are five points of similarity —, characteristics common to the two passages. They seem to me too striking to be the work of chance and too natural to make it at all improbable that the poet had in mind the same order of the hierarchy of angels in the Elene as in the Crist. The contradiction between the Elene narrative and the Genesis account (Gen. 3:24) which the poet would naturally try to reproduce is further proof of this.

The Angels are the victorious race siȝorcynn (E. v. 754). The hosts of angels that accompanied the miraculous phenomena that were manifest at Guthlac's death sang the song of victory. enȝla preatas siȝeleoð sunȝon (G. v. 1288 f.). May not this conception of the angels as a victorious host, a triumphant race, which has overcome the machinations of evil and enjoys the compensation of victory have been suggested by the blissful condition of the heroes who receive their reward amid the joys of Walhalla?

6. DEVIL.

From the angels the messengers of God and of Light we turn our attention to the devils, the messengers of Evil and Darkness. The devil presented in these poems was the ambitious rebel in heaven before he fell according to God's decree; he became, after the fall, the enemy of human happiness and the constant opposer of God's beneficent plan on earth. He is given a large number of descriptive and characteristic names, each of which designates him by emphasizing some particular phase of his character or by making prominent some part of his nature. He is called by the christian poet the accursed wolf[1], the beast of dark deeds se awyrȝda wulf . . . . deor dædscua (C. v. 256 f.). He is the baleful one se bealofulla (C. v. 259) who severely oppresses christians and holds them in confinement; further, he is the dark spirit which at first seduced and misled man, se swearta ȝæst (C. v. 269 f.), the injurer of the people þam leodsceaðan (C. v. 273), the malignant destroyer sceððendum sceaðan (C. v. 1396), hellsceaðan (E. v. 956). The devil that appeared to Juliana is addressed by her

---

[1]) An interesting parallel to C. v. 256 f. is found in the Marien Himmelfahrt, Haupt's Ztschr. V, S. 520, z. 190 f. 'do der vil vngehöre hellewolf' etc.

in a list of derogatory designations each of which seems to vie with all the others in the expression of base and despicable qualities. He is not only the rebel against God but the oppressor of men as well *haleða gewinna* (J. v. 243), and of souls (J. v. 555); he is experienced in evil *yfles andwis* (J. v. 244), the prisoner of hell *helle hæftling* (J. v. 246). As the one deprived of his heavenly abode he is the banished one *se wrecmæcʒa* (J. v. 260), as the one who raised opposition in heaven he is *waldres wiðerbreca* (J. v. 269), the originator of sin *fyrnsynna fruman* (J. v. 347) and the worker of evil *wrohtes wyrhtan* (J. v. 346). His general hostility to all things good and to mankind is summed up in the term *feond* (E. v. 953) of mankind *mancynnes* (J. v. 630), of souls *sawla* (J. v. 348). He is further the perfidious exile *wræcca wærleas* (J. v. 351), the wretched unclean spirit *earmsceapen unclæne ʒæst* (J. v. 418), the covenant breaker *þam wærloʒan* (J. v. 455), the abject spirit of hell *hean helle ʒæst* (J. v. 457). Satan himself is the ruler of his cohorts, he stands at the head of his kind, is the king of hell's inhabitants *cyninʒ hellwara* (J. v. 544), the malicious lord of murder *manfrea morðres* (J. v. 546), the instigator of crime *manes melda* (J. v. 557) and the *synna brytta* (E. v. 957), as the Deity was the *boldes brytta* (E. v. 162).

In antithesis to the angels which were white, gleaming, and glorious in appearance, the devil is a hateful, dark, black spirit (C. v. 269, 897 f.), and as the former were the messengers of God to perform his missions so the latter are the servants of their father, satan. The devil which approached the holy Juliana was a subject, a son indeed, delegated by his overlord and father to make this journey to her:

Hwæt mec min fæder   on þas fore to þe
hellwarena cyninʒ   hider onsende   (J. v. 321 f.)

The devil relates to Juliana that the king of the inhabitants of hell sends his messengers out on their missions of evil and that unless successful in the task assigned them, they return with great fear to his presence because of the punishment that there awaits them (J. v. 325 ff.). As Juliana's faith was anchored to the God of glory, so the devil's hope was established in the infernal king (J. v. 436 f.). The devil, clutched by Juliana and interrogated, relates a long series of crimes and evils which he has instigated and adds that he may not, though he sit the summerlong day, relate all the crimes which he in the course of time has, in sin, performed:

                      I asecȝan ne mæȝ
  þeah ic ȝesitte   sumerlonȝne dæȝ
  eal þa earfeðu   þe ic ær and sið
  ȝefremede to faene   (J. v. 494 ff.).

Not only the individual devil but also the hosts of hell's inhabitants *hellwarena heap* (C. v. 731) are mentioned. The enmity existing between the King of Heaven and the king of hell and his subjects is strong and centers about the spiritual rule of the earth as the prize of the contest. The description of the strife for authority, the retaking from the power of the devil the hosts of those who had been won through deceit, bears many characteristics of a real strife in Anglosaxon military life. Christ wages a personal combat against his old foes *ealdfiondum* (C. v. 567) and robs hell of the tribute *þæs ȝafoles* which it in the days of old basely gorged in the strife. He bore off the greatest booty *huða mæste* (C. v. 568) from the city *byriȝ* (C. v. 569) of his foes; an unnumbered folk: He bound their king in fiery bonds and left him imprisoned in fetters and bars (C. v. 732 f.)[1]. The whole narrative here is teeming with such war terms as are common to the description of such conflicts as are depicted in Judith and Byrhtnoð's Death, and the description here must be admitted to posses all the characteristics of the description of an actual visible conflict between mortal physical foes.

The devil that came to Juliana had the form of an angel *hæfde enȝles hiw* (J. v. 244), and was an air-navigating being *lyft lacende* (J. v. 281). These characteristics may or may not evince his former character as an angel, for in Elene the devil that appeared to Judas was also a flying being *on lyft astah* (E. v. 899), and the devils that came to St. Guthlac were able to assume various forms (G. v. 866 ff.). Special stress is laid

---

[1] For a representation of Satan bound in fetters see the illustration to the Cædmon Mss. published by Ellis, Archeologia XXIV.

upon three things respecting the devils that came to St. Guthlac:
they came in crowds; they were noisy and uproarious; they were
able to change their forms. They came to him in a host (vs.
866), in troops thronging (v. 868); they were a death-bearing
crowd (vs. 867) and spoke in a variety of ways and with many
voices (v. 870), sometimes uttering a scream, a loud war cry
bludne hereeirm (v. 872), sometimes raving like wild beasts *hwilum
wedende swa wilde deor* (v. 879). Sometimes they assumed the
appearance of human beings *hwilum cyrdon . . . . on mennisc hiw*
(v. 880 f.); sometimes they changed themselves into the form of
a worm or serpent *hwilum bru͵don . . . . on wyrmes bleo* and
spat poison *attre spiowdon* (v. 884). Kemble cites two passages
from Salomon and Saturn in which the same characteristics of
the devil are noted which we find here, and adds that the passages
are redolent of heathenism[1]).

The designation of the devil as *se aglæca* (J. v. 268, 319,
E. v. 901) probably conveyed the conception of a monster, or
mighty evil-working spirit; the same word designates the dragon
in Beo. (v. 2535, 2906), and also refers to Grendel (v. 593).

Attention has often enough been called to the similarity of
the role which Loki plays in the Baldr myth and that which Lucifer
plays in the story of the rebellion in heaven against the authority
of God. I need only note that the parallelism called attention to by
Kemble[2]) and others has been minutely investigated by Bugge[3])
in connection with the christian Early English poems among which
are noted especially Crist and Juliana. Bugge has compared carefully
the parallelism in the general narrative and in the traits of character
of the two beings and his conclusion is that the christian poems
are the source of those colorings in the myth which bear similarities
with christian teaching. "Denn Loki ist seinem Ursprung nach der
Lucifer des christlichen Mittelalters, doch so, dass dieser als Loki
in sich Elemente von Merkur, Apollo, Eris und mehreren andern
antiken Mythusfiguren aufgenommen hat".

[1]) Kemble S. in E. I. p. 388 f.
[2]) Ibid. p. 382.
[3]) Bugge, Entstehung der nordischen Götter und Heldensagen S. 53 ff.

The devil of these poems, whether represented as ruler, fiend, son, monster, fallen angel or air-navigating being in the form of an angel; a creature able to assume the form of a repulsive serpent or an animal of hideous proportions; a spirit striving to accomplish all evil and work all harm against God and men, is, in its main outlines, the devil of Judaic teaching, but with the addition of such traits and elements as the enthusiasm for the new religion coupled with gross fanaticism would naturally produce. To make more prominent the salient features of his Satanic majesty, to clothe him with all imaginable hideous traits — some of them doubtless interwoven with untraceable heathen beliefs, was to bring into the service of the new belief a more striking, more concrete, more real devil the product of both Scriptural teaching and the devices of a prolific phantasy.

7. HELL.

The hell which may be depicted from material found in Crist Juliana and Elene bears some characteristics of the Norse conception of Hel, the cold and cheerless region over which the goddess of the same name held sway[1], the region of death; hades, the invisible. It is too in some respects like Nastrond, the place filled with torments for the perjurer and the secret murderer[2]. Biblical teaching of course furnishes most of the material whence the whole conception is drawn. In general we may say that the biblical conceptions are more prominent in Crist, the heathen conceptions in Juliana and Elene, while Guthlac and Fata Apostolorum furnish little of interest to the theme.

Hell is represented as the narrow home *þam engan ham* (J. v. 323, E. v. 920), referring doubtless to a state of confinement, a condition especially abhorrent to the Anglosaxon mind: the expressions *hæftned* (E. v. 297), and *helle hæftling* J. v. 246) are in accord with this significance of *engan ham*. It is further the dark, gloomy home *þam þystran ham* (J. v. 683), the dwelling of the condemned *wearhtreafum* (E. v. 926), the court of darkness *heolstorhofu* (E. v. 763), the court of sadness *þam gnornhofe* (J. v.

---

[1] Kemble S. in E. I, p. 392.
[2] Ibid. p. 393.

324). Hell is conceived of as a house *susla hus* (C. v. 1604), *witchus* (C. v. 1536), entered by a door *helle duru* (E. v. 1230) and as a hall of death *deaðsele* (G. v. 1048) whose inmates bereft of all joys and plagued by various torments drag out a sorrowful existence. As the angels and their king inhabited a *burʒ*, so the abode of the devils is graphically called the city of fiends in *hyriʒ fionda* (J. v. 545. C. v. 569).

Perhaps the description in Julana v. 681 ff. has as little of the christian conception of hell as any in the poems. The narrative is of the disastrous voyage of Helisens and his thirty-four companions, after the martyrdom of Juliana. The poet says: deprived of joy and without hope they sought hell, nor may the thanes in that dark home, the assembly of companions in that deep cavern expect from their prince the rich possessions of the living — that they in the wine-hall at the beer benches shall receive rings appled gold . . . .

                hroðra bidæled
hyhta lease   helle sohton
ne þorftan þa þeʒnas   in þam þystran ham
seo ʒeneatscolu   in þam neolan scræfe
to þam frumʒare   feohʒestealda
witedra wenan,   þæt hy in winsele
ofer beorsetle   beaʒas þeʒon.
applede ʒold!   (J. v. 681 ff.)

This is not the hell of christian teaching, but that joyless state characteristic of the heathen realm of Hel. It is noteworthy that here one of the woes — and the one made most prominent — is the lack of that which was so highly prized by the loyal Anglosaxon, viz. the possibility of meeting with his companions about the drinking benches in the mead-hall and of there being recognized and honored by his lord in token of particular merit or distinguished services.

The hell to which the unrighteous are condemned after the Day of Judgment does not show so much evidence of the influence of heathen beliefs, yet is by no means free from traces of them. It is represented as a deep abyss *deope dæl* (C. v. 1532), *susla ʒrund* (E. v. 913) containing a swart flame *swartne liʒ* (C. v. 1533), a leaping flame *lacende lig* (E. v. 580) which shall dissolve the bodies of those coming in contact with it *hra bryttað* (E. v. 579). Those condemned to hell shall not escape their sins but bound in the flames they shall suffer death *lege gebundne; swylt prowiað* (C. v. 1539). Such stress is laid upon the perpetuity of this death and the horrors of its consummation, and so vivid is the whole picture that I cannot forbear to insert the lines from C. v. 1541—49 which afford one of the liveliest descriptions in the whole poem. The content is this: That is eternal death; nor may that hot abyss throughout the everlasting night to all eternity avail to burn away the sin from that infernal race, the stain from their souls; but there the deep pit nourishes the sad ones, bottomless, it guards the spirits in its gloom; it burns them with its old flame and with its terrible cold, consumes them with its hateful serpents and many punishments, with terrible nourishment (?) inflicts injury upon the folk.

<pre>
            þæt is ece cwealm!
ne mæᵹ þæt hate dæl   of heolodcynne
in synnehte   synne forbærnan
to widan feore,   wom of þære sawle
ac þær se deopa seað   dreorᵹe fedeð
ᵹrundleas ᵹiemeð   ᵹæsta on þeostre
aleð hy mid þy ealdan liᵹe and mid þy eᵹsan forste,
wraðum wyrmum and mid wita fela
frecnum feorhᵹomum folcum scendeð.
</pre>

Here are distinct traces of heathen beliefs. Such antitheses as are contained in the idea of the presence of heat and cold, flame and darkness in one and the same place are not biblical teaching. The same idea is found elsewhere in Anglosaxon poetry e. g. Genesis (v. 43); Salomon and Saturn (v. 467 f.) exhibits thoughts parallel with those in the lines above cited, but with more prominence give to the feature of coldness in the enumeration of hell's torments.

The subjects for punishment suffer the hottest of fires *hattost headowelma* (E. v. 579) in a place of destruction *forwyrd* (E. v. 764), endure slavery *þeowned þolian* (E. v. 769), in a place of the blackest and most terrible punishments *in þa sweartestan and þa wyrrestan witebroȝan* (E. v. 930 f.); they suffer the qualms of death in the embrace of the dragon *dreoȝað deaðewale in dracan fiðme* (E. v. 764 ff). This occurs in the description of the fall of the angels and obviously *dracan* cannot refer to the devil as he did not as yet exist. The expression is here doubtless the conception adopted by popular fancy, of the mouth of a monstrous beast which served as the entrance to the place of torment. This appears from the illustrations of the Caedmon MSS[1]).

The doomed ones shall dwell in the bath of fire *on fyrbaðe* (E. v. 948), and placed on a lighted funeral pyre, they shall endure the curse and misery without end (E. v. 950 f.) Yet notwithstanding the fact that they are in the surge of the fire *wylme* (E. v. 764), the inmates of hell are at the same time in shadowy darkness [*prostratum forðglmed*] (E. v. 764 f.).

The statement that hell shall then take the host of the perfidious ones *þonne hel nimeð werleasra weorud* (C. v. 1613 f.) recalls the goddess whom mythology names as the governess in hell. In the lines above inserted *seað* is also in like manner personified and is spoken of as having the care of the spirits in its darkness.

[1]) Archaeologia. XXIV, Plates LV and LXII.

III. THE STATE.

The Anglosaxon political and social condition in the eighth century was at such a degree of primitiveness as to make the application of the modern term 'state' to it almost unsuitable; yet we are at a loss for a better term to designate in a comprehensive sense the civic community of that period; and we may perhaps so divest ourselves of our modern ideas that the application of the word state may with sufficient clearness designate the collective civic relations of that primitive society — the whole forming in a generic sense a state.

With this generic significance then we use the term and shall collect in this section of the essay whatever we may find relative to the state, or more specifically, the suggestions relative to the ruler and the ruled, the functions of each, their reciprocal relations, their conjunctive action to meet national ends, as in war, assemblies etc. We shall note here too whatever suggestions we may find relative to the social and family life of the Anglosaxon, as being integral factors in the collective body we are pleased to call the state.

It is to be borne in mind that the Cynewulfian poems are poetical elaborations of prose Latin legends and homilies and that whatever appears in the Anglosaxon without addition or diminution as it stood in the Latin does not properly form a part of our theme. Juliana, Guthlac and Elene, based upon selections from the Acta Sanctorum, are not of a character to yield very extensively to our purpose, while Crist from the nature of the whole will yield even less, for there is almost nothing except the allusions to the character and attributes of a ruler in the anthropomorphic references to Christ, and the reciprocal relation of king and subject as transferred to Christ and his disciples.

1. RULER.

We consider first the tribal or national ruler, the king; and here we are restricted almost exclusively to material in Juliana and Elene, to what is said of Maximian, Heliseus, Constantine and Helen.

The Anglosaxon monarch was before all else a military hero. It could scarcely be otherwise in a land divided into petty principalities each striving for prominence and able to win and maintain such prominence only through excellence in military operations. Under such circumstances the head of each principality must of necessity be a warrior able to lead and command men. An examination of the titles given to the ruler proves the high estimation in which military qualities were held. Maximian's Latin title is imperator and is translated simply *cyning*, but immediately after is added the title *hildfruma* (J. v. 7) as though naming him from his most important attribute. Constantine is given the same name (E. v. 10) and from this *hildfruma* he was raised to leader of the army *heretema* (E. v. 10). The word used here *ahæfen*, 'raised' alludes perhaps to the ceremony of installing the king when he was raised upon a shield and exhibited to the multitude which greeted him with acclamations[1]. The king was skillful on the battle field, nimble in the use of the shield *lindhwata* (E. v. 11), actively engaging in the pitched battle *heaðofremmende* (E. v. 130), himself displaying bravery *niðheard cyning* (E. v. 195), able in the fight *guðheard* (E. v. 204), bold with the spear *garþrist* (E. v. 204). Thus, although he was leader of the host *hererœsua* (E. v. 994), he possessed the valorous qualities of the common soldier as well and took active part in the contest. As a distinguished military hero Cynewulf gives him many appellations drawn from war, its preparations and results. He is the protector of the people *leodgebyrga* (E. v. 11, 203), the battle guardian for his men *guðweard gumena* (E. v. 14), and their protection *wigena hleo* (E. v. 150) *æðelinga hleo* (E. v. 99), the king famous in battle *heaðurof cyning* (E. v. 152). He was the helmet of the army *herigu helm* (E. v. 148, 223) whose presence was a surety and

[1] Kemble S. in E. I. p. 154.

protection to the army as the helmet rendered the head of the warrior secure. The king was the guardian of his own realm *rices hyrde* (J. v. 66).

After the din of battle had ceased the king bestowed presents as rewards or tokens of esteem and honor upon subjects who in some manner had merited his royal attention, and from this custom he is given such titles as *beorna beaᵹᵹifa* (E. v. 100, 1198) the spender of rings, or the gold-distributing friend of the men *goldwine gumena* (E. v. 201), the distributor of treasure *sinces bryltta* (E. v. 194) and the granter of wishes *wilᵹifa* (E. v. 221). The Cynewulfian poems do not present in this respect any example of the generous king as e. g. Hroðᵹar is represented in Beo. 1021 ff.

The foregoing have been war titles: what were the civil titles of the Anglosaxon monarch? Constantine the emperor *casere* (E. v. 42, 70, etc.) is called the *riht cyninᵹ* (v. 13) of mighty fame *tireadiᵹ* (E. v. 104): as significant of the dignity and wisdom of age he is the *foles* or *seᵹa aldor* (E. v. 157, 97): considered as the acme of the social and political classes of his state he is the first of men *leodfruma* (E. v. 191): representing him as one sprung from the ranks of his own people, he is the prince *peoden* (J. v. 82, 86, etc., E. v. 267): he is also the *hlaford* of his people (E. v. 265, J. v. 129).

The foregoing war and peace titles are all given to Constantine, a king, highest officer. In Heliseus we have an under-officer, perhaps the second in rank to the king. His Roman title is generally praefectus. The Latin narrative runs: erat quidam Senator in civitate Nicomedia nomine Eleusius: and again: dedit munera Imperatori Maximiano et successit Praefecto alio administranti, seditque in carruca agens officium Praefecturae. These references to the Acta Sanctorum give us the official position of Heliseus which was that of Prefect or Governor of a province holding his position of civil and military leader at the pleasure of the emperor and representing the latter in the far-off Asia minor province. Our poet often speaks of him in terms elsewhere applied to the king himself, but the terminology usually implies that he is a subordinate officer. He is the reeve of the kingdom rice *ʒerefa*¹) (J. v. 19. 530), a warrior of lofty personal courage *se hererinc* (J. v. 189), the folkleader *folctoʒa* (J. v. 225) closely allied to *heretoʒa* which Kemble observes is the proper name for the officer next in rank to the king²); *heretoʒa* is his name however as ruler and leader of the army and is often replaced by ealdorman to denote his civil position. Nowhere in the poem is Heliseus spoken of as ealdorman though this is the name we might expect the poet to have given to the ruler of a ducal estate or *ealdordom* as his estate is called *hwfile ealdordom micelne and mærne* (J. v. 25. 190). Significant of the attachment and esteem felt for the ruler is the title *monna leofast* (J. v. 84). To Heliseus is ascribed yet another prerogative in the title *se dema* (J. v. 591. 602). The prerogatives just noted are such as have been shown elsewhere to be connected with the idea of royalty³). The judicial function was rarely ascribed to the king. In Juliana *se dema* is not a translation from the Latin but an appellation voluntarily assigned by the poet. That the king did exercise the function of judge sometimes and that he may, in a sense, be considered to have been the highest judicial officer we learn from Kemble; but the exercise of his right except in extreme cases or in answer to a last appeal, was unusual⁴). The ealdorman was the principal judicial officer in his province or shire⁵) and so the poet in his use of *dema* employs a term which is not only decriptive of the part which Heliseus acts in the narrative but is also consistent with the office of *ealdorman* or ruler of the shire to whom in a general way the Roman prefect corresponds. The term *dema* may have been associated in the poet's mind with *ʒerefa* an officer who undoubtedly exercised the prerogatives of judge.

Almost inseparable from position of honor and dignity was wealth and high birth. Heliseus is wealthy *whtwdiʒ* (J. v. 18), *se weliʒa* (J. v. 38. 569) *ʒoldspediʒ ʒuma* (J. v. 39), has riches

¹) Cf. Kemble S. in E. II, p. 151 and 169.
²) Ibid. p. 125.
" Cf. Rau, Alterthümer in Exodus p. 23; Ferrell, Antiquities in Genesis p. 31; Kent p. 30.
⁴ Cf. Kemble S. in E. II, ch. III, IV, and V, and Grimm, Deutsche Rechtsalterthümer, Göttingen 1828, p. 752 ff.
⁵) Kemble, ibid. p 134.

under the treasure lock *feoh҄gestreon under hordlocan* (J. v. 12) and numberless precious ornaments *hyrsta unrim* (J. v. 43). Juliana's father urges as a reason that she should accept the ruler's proffers, that he is richer in treasure than she *ahtspedi҄gra feoh҄gestreona* (J. v. 101). The possession of wealth and treasures was indispensable for the chieftain who must repay distinguished service with gifts, must be a *bea҄g҄gifa* or *sinces brytta*.

The high birth of Heliseus is also strongly emphasized; he is of noble birth, comes of noble stock *æðeles cynnes* (J. v. 18) and is a hero of noble qualities *beorn* (J. v. 41).

In all the essentials of royalty the queen mother, Helen, rises to the dignity of a ruling prince: she is commissioned by the emperor to go on the long expedition in search of the cross and her position as governess of the retinue and folk with her, as presiding officer of the assemblies held, leads the poet to designate her as one clothed with all the prerogatives of royalty. The thought of her at the head of an expedition probably influenced the poet to call her the war-queen *guðcwen* (E. v. 254), and the victorious queen *si҄gcwen* (E. v. 260) known to fame *tirædi҄g* (E. v. 605) although in the account of her actions she is involved in no warfare; yet her position at the head of an expedition and the instinctive connection between lofty military and political rank which seems to have existed in the poet's mind gave to the appellations of royalty even the impress of war and battle. Under various other appellations is she referred to e. g. *seo cwen* (E. v. 662), the lady *hlæfdi҄ge* (E. v. 656), relation of the emperor, *caseres mæ҄g* (E. v. 669).

The description of enthroned royalty in E. v. 329 ff. is the only one in Elene, in short in the Cynewulfian poems, and possesses no little interest. The stately war queen *gealtolic guðcwen* sits in splendor *prymme* upon the royal throne *in cynestole*, the relation of the emperor adorned with gold *caseres mæ҄g .... golde gehyrsted*, as the crowds press about her and as president of the assembly she states its purpose and opens the discussion. Kent seems to me rightly to infer that this glimpse of reigning royalty upon a chair of state and with the pomp and splendor of imperial majesty was no doubt a reflection of some more vivid picture in the poet's own mind of the brilliant scenes of indigenous courts and hospitable mead halls.

Some expressions found in Crist evidently drawn from phases of Anglosaxon royalty, but alluding to the Deity are *helm* (C. v. 566, 634), the protector of warriors *wiʒendra hleo* (C. v. 409), the distributer of breasure *sincʒiefa* (C. v. 460), a term associated with the custom previously alluded to of bestowing presents upon warriors, courtiers or minstrels; *wilʒiefa* (C. v. 537) granter of desires, referring probably to the same custom; guardian of the kingdom *rices weard* (C. v. 1528), of the people *folces* (C. v. 1647), of victory (C. v. 1517, 243).

A presentation of court life with its ceremonies and formalities such as are presented in the narrative of Beowulf's visit to Hroðgar's court, his reception by the warden, his admittance at last to the king himself is entirely lacking in the Cynewulfian poems.

2. THE RULED.

In the great body of the folk over whom the King exercised the highest executive authority are to be distinguished different classes of subjects. Since our data affords us only a few glimpses of this aspect of the state it will be impossible to state with certainty much about these classes, their relative rank, their relation to each other, or their rights and privileges.

The Etheling *æðelinʒ* evidently belonged to a high, perhaps the highest, class of nobility. Heliseus the ruler of an *ealdordom* is quite frequently called *æðelinʒ* (J. v. 37, 58, 164), so is Constantine the emperor also (E. v. 12, 202). The Anglosaxon nomenclature carried into the realm of religious thought gives to Christ the same title (C. v. 158, 448, 627 etc.); the dignity of his rank is still further exalted by making him the *æðelinʒa ord* (C. v. 515, 846 etc.); to Constantine is assigned the rank *æðelinʒa hleo* (E. v. 99). Who are meant by the *æðelinʒas* in these instances? In Elene v. 845 ff. *æðelinʒas* seems to be used synonymously with *fiðe ʒeslas* and *eorlas*, those in immediate attendance upon the queen herself. This would naturally justify the conclusion that they were a select few, chosen upon some principle of birth, natural endowments or excellence achieved through skill or industry forming a class whose head was the monarch himself.

The term *eorl* varies in its meaning in our poems, signifying, I take it, as well one of distinguished rank as men in general without exacter reference to station. In J. v. 512 we may understand it as applying to the ruler and his surrounding attendants, while J. v. 510, C. v. 516, 875 exhibit its use as a term for men in general. C. v. 510 it is a translation of *hominibus*. Guthlac is the *eorl ellenheard* (v. 1138) and is yet further distinguished among earls as the *eorla wyn* (v. 1179). In Elene those about the queen are named *eorlas* as well as *æðelingas*. The band that accompanied the queen in search of the cross consisted of earls (E. v. 225, 275.) The three thousand Jews constituting the first assembly which Helen called are also called earls (E. v. 321) but these were selected upon a principle of excellence *þa þe deoplicost dryhtnes geryno .... recean cuðon* (E. v. 280 f.). The second assembly of one thousand Jews was likewise a body of earls (E. v. 332) and these again were distinguished by some trait, were *wisfæste weras wordes cræftige* etc. (E. v. 314). The third assembly of five hundred consisted also of earls (E. v. 404), those who best knew the writings of old *þa þe fyrngewritu þurh snyttro cræft selest cunnen* (E. v. 373 f.). Judas the *eorla hleo* was of noble stock *æðeles cynnes* (E. v. 59), *wordcræftes wis ond witgan sunu* (E. v. 592). The same word designates the Jews in general (E. v. 435). In all these uses of the word the idea of excellence of some sort is the constant factor. They were subjects whose privilege apparently it was to be near their monarch, often doubtless in the capacity of stalwart warriors, famed for prowess in war, and in time of peace occupying a social position of superior rank forming a step in the existing germ of the Feudal System, although in these poems there are no hints at a mastery over a lower rank of society. Respecting the relative rank of earl and etheling our data affords small means of determining, yet the frequency with which *æðeling* is applied to Heliseus Constantine and Christ while *eorl* is rarely so used implies strongly the preeminence of the former class.

The allusions to other ranks of society are little more than verbal. The courtiers, perhaps menials, about the king who await his will in the performance of service are the þegnas (J. v 12, 683) a band of followers whom the poet characterizes as pryðfulle (J. v. 12); they constitute an escort geneatscolu (J. v. 684) and are often the recipients of his generosity (J. v. 684 f.). It is their privilege in event of certain celebrations to assemble about their lord in the wine-hall at the tables and there to pass the time in festive drinking, and to receive tokens from the hand of their lord himself commending their services and at the same time clothing them with honor, as we are warranted in inferring from the negative assertion in J. v. 683 ff. The same custom is referred to in the words of Affricanus to Heliseus *et þe þine hyldu winburgum in* (J. v. 82 f.) which contains also an occult suggestion of the worth attached by the subject to the approbation and favor of his prince. In Elene the þegna heap is spoken of as being present at the assembly of people *heremeðle* (E. v. 549). This was the assembly of Jews which was afterwards dismissed and Judas alone retained to answer the queen's questions (E. v. 598 f.). Helen then directed her conversation to him alone *þam anhagan* (E. v. 604); he replies, and she again speaks openly before the earls *for eorlum* (E. v. 620). Who is meant by the earls here is not clear, but most likely the reference is to her continual escort consisting probably of thanes i. e. servants, and of earls, noblemen; and this body, her retinue is called once the þegna heap (E. v. 549) and once the earls (E. v. 620). Constantine had such an escort þegna þreat (E. v. 154). this, however, was a war-band.

Designating the great body of the populace of which we learn little are *werþeod* (E. v. 17. 643), *folc* (E. v. 1094) *leod* E. v. 128. 468 ; and signifying men in general are *firas* (J. v. 218. G. v. 961. C. v. 35); *elde* (J. v. 727. G. v. 793. C. v. 582); *wer* is the individual with fixed value as in (J. v. 300. G. v. 897); it is also used in a broad general sense (cf. C. v. 416. 634. 1048 etc.). In Crist v. 37. 419 it means husband; *beorn* has the general meaning mankind in J. v. 272. C. v. 992. but the more usual signification of hero, chief or leader in (C. v. 449. 530); *guma* (J. v. 39). (E. v. 638); *hæleð* (E. v. 538); *secg* (E. v. 552) also occur with more or less frequency. The difference in the use and meaning of these words is not evident enough to enable us to draw distinctions or make classifications. It is the same variety of expression which is so common everywhere in Anglosaxon poetry and is well exhibited in the various expressions for sea, crowd, ruler, ship etc., words constantly used and names of things most familiar to the speaker. A fine example of the characteristic Anglosaxon shading and one which gives us at the same time a glimpse of Anglo-Germanic usage is the passage J. v. 58—68. The Latin original says: audiens haec Praefectus vocavit patrem eius et dixit ei omnia verba quae ei mandaverat Juliana. The poet has re-wrought this into the description of the summoning of an Anglosaxon subject to an interview and the conference of the ruler with him. The summoning of Juliana's father is done through the messenger *ærend* who brings him immediately to the conference *to rune*. The interview pictured is between two stalwart Germanic warriors *hildeþremman*; after they have leaned their spears together *siððan hy toʒædre ʒaras hlændon*[1]), the deliberation proceeds. The guardian of the kingdom, as is fitting, speaks first and adds emphasis to his utterances by an occasional flourish of his javelin *darod hæbbende*.

From this suggestion of a deliberative council or interview it is an easy transition to the real assemblies which are mentioned in Elene. These it is true throw little light upon the real Anglosaxon assembly, the *witena ʒemot* or meeting of the wise men who came together about their sovereign in his *burʒ* or in open air about a familiar tree or perhaps before the file of battle to deliberate upon matters of grave importance for the realm; for they are here purely ecclesiastical in purpose and the poet has in general been true to his Latin source. Four different assemblies are called: the first called by Constantine and presided over by him consists of the wisest *þa wisestan* who were acquainted with the old writings and from whom he demanded information respecting the miraculous sign and the god it signified (E. v. 153 f.). The other assemblies of three thousand, one thousand and five-hundred Jews respectively were summoned at Helen's bidding and presided over by her (E. v. 282, 326, 377 f.). The queen

---

[1]) Cf. with this the description of the arrival of Beowulf and his companions at Hroðgar's court. Beow. 328 ff.

throned in majesty (E. v. 329 f.) each time introduces the deliberations. Finally the assembly of Jews is done away with entirely and the queen demands of Judas alone the desired information. These assemblies of Jews selected for their wisdom and learning are rather in the nature of conventions than of the *gemots* of the Anglosaxon wise men whose numbers must have been much less as we know that it sometimes met in a single room[1]).

3. PUNISHMENT.

The narration of the punishment of Juliana and Judas affords us some interesting suggestions as to the methods of inflicting penal discipline. Some hints may be gleaned also from the poetical representations of hell which, as is well known, is often likened to a prison.

The poet has told us more about imprisonment than any other mode of inflicting punishment and this mainly in Juliana and Elene, doubtless owing to the incidents of the stories found in his sources and influenced also perhaps by the fact that imprisonment was the most usual punishment prescribed in the code of penalties with which he was acquainted. He has modified the Latin carcer into the Anglosaxon prison cell which is styled the narrow court *þam engan hofe* (J. v. 532). It should be recalled that hell was represented as the narrow home *þam engan ham* (J. v. 323) and that the state of imprisonment intensified greatly the general distress of the infernal regions. Juliana's prison was further a compulsion room *nydclafa* (J. v. 240), a place where the wills of the obstreperous and stubborn were subdued. It was a locked house *hlinreced* (J. v. 243), enveloped in darkness *heolstre biþelmad* (J. v. 241). Judas was cast into a pit *in drygne seað* (in lacum siccum) to spend seven nights in hard imprisonment under *hearmlocan* (E. v. 695) and to be oppressed with hunger *hungre gepreatad* v. 695), he was moreover bound in fetters *clommum beclungen*, and on the seventh day he was weakened with pain, tired and hungry. Kent (p. 41) justly affirms "that the lack of any sustenance *meteleas* is particularly emphasized as the most intolerable feature of the torture, for this is given as

---

[1] Cf. Kemble H. p. 200.

the ground of his desire for release, that he was worn out by the enmity of hunger *heanne from hungres geniðlan* and that hunger prevents him from resisting longer"; but I can not see that his (Kent's) conclusion that 'this varied and repeated reference to hunger as a part of the punishment by confinement must have been based upon an existing actuality in the punishment of the day' follows either as a necessity or even as a clear probability. Kent seems to have overlooked the Latin source to which, I take it, the references to hunger are due rather than to the reflections on the poet's mind of any 'existing actuality in the punishment of the day'. Helen took an oath to starve Judas to death 'per crucifixum, fame te interficiam' *le þæt gesweri3e .... þæt þu hungre scealt .... cwylmed weorðan* (E. v. 686) if he did not reveal to her the truth about the cross. This is part of the Latin narrative and in his development of the plan of the poem it is only natural that the poet's mind should revert especially to the means, viz hunger by which Judas was to be put to death if he persisted in his stubbornness; for in both the Latin and the Anglosaxon the imprisonment seems to have been the *means* of executing the punishment by hunger rather than that the hunger was an *incident* of the punishment by imprisonment. Perhaps Grimm's omission of hunger in his list of the punishments among the German races need not after all be considered so "strange".

Respecting capital punishment also there is an interesting reference in Juliana where the deviation from the original is such as gives a strong suggestion at least about some things respecting the manner of an Anglosaxon execution. The poet says that Juliana was conducted near to the landmark *londmearce neah* (J. v. 635), to the place where they intended to put her to death etc. Kemble in his discussion of the Mark[1]) points out that it was, as the name denotes, a division of land maked out, having settled boundaries, inhabited and cultivated by freemen. In its restricted sense it was a boundary and was under the protection of the gods[2]) and also under the safe guard of public law[3]), vigorously

[1]) S. in E. I, p. 35 f.
[2]) Kemble, I. p. 43.
[3]) Ibid., p. 46.

shielded from violation It had a certain sanctity that might not with impunity be violated, for on the maintenance of that sanctity depended the safety of the community and the regular service of the deities that presided over the common weal. If as Kemble thinks[1]) the execution among early Germanic peoples was in the nature of a sacrifice to the gods, where could that sacrifice be with more propriety offered than on the land-mark, the ground especially sacred to them? In Juliana's case, whose sin was partially, at least, in the obstinate adherence to a god not recognized among the deities of her people, the execution on the ground associated with rejected deities would lend emphasis to the example of which she was made. The method of inflicting capital punishment here used, *þurh sweordslege* (J. v. 671) is one of the methods discussed by Grimm[2]) as being in vogue early in England.

4. WAR AND WARRIORS.

The military or war force was very closely identified with the state in the thought of the Anglosaxon; its efficiency might indicate the relative rank of the petty Anglosaxon kingdoms whose prestige dated from a single successful campaign or whose history closed with a military disaster. The large number of terms descriptive of different aspects of war, diffused so generally throughout the whole range of Anglosaxon poetry, is clear and convincing proof of the important role it played in the life and thought of the race. That it was so important and that the poetry so distinctly reflects it is a natural consequence of the relations existing among the Anglosaxon principalities at the period when poetical literature flourished. The Cynewulfian poems with the exception of the Elene yield as little perhaps to this subject as any of the longer poems in the literature — a natural result of the themes treated. Aside from the contest with the barbarians depicted in Elene the poet depicts no war preparations, describes no actual campaign, portrays no real fight and presents no warring hero as such to afford scope for the war vocabulary and the vivid narration which occur in many other pieces; but in spite of this,

[1]) Kemble I, p. 47, n. 3.
[2]) Deutsche Rechtsalterthümer S. 689.

a theme with which he is so intimate must show itself at times and so Juliana and Guthlac offer many war terms and suggestions. The second part of Crist is also relatively rich in them¹).

We have seen that the ruler was a war chieftain engaging actively in the battle and accepting the dangers of the common soldier. The earls and ethelings were the attendants of his standard acting in the capacity of the common soldier (E. v. 66). So also on the expedition of Helen which was in many respects equipped as a war expedition, the immediate attendants of the queen are designated as *æscrofe eorlas* (E. v. 275). Thus the king, ethelings, earls, were fully represented in the rank and file of battle. Designating the great mass of warriors are often the ordinary terms for man as *secʒas*, *weras* etc., but more specifically the man as warrior is *cempa* (J. v. 17, 290), *wiʒa* (C. v. 985. E. v. 150). *wiʒend* (E. v. 106). *Rinc* and *beorn* have the stronger meaning of hero (E. v. 46, 114).

Collectively considered the army is the *here* (E. v. 32), the battle host *beaduþreat* (E. v. 31); the *feðan* (E. v. 35) primarily the infantry, and this meaning suits very well here if we accept Körner's translation of *coreðcestum* "ausgewählte reiterschaar". The warriors are variously named from some attribute or incident as the lancewarriors *dearoðlæcende* (E. v. 37), the war-companions *guðʒelacan* (E. v. 43); those who stand shoulder to shoulder in the rank of battle sharing a common weal or woe *eorlʒesteallan* (E. v. 64); the battle heroes *hilderincas*, *fyrdrincas* (E. v. 261, 263), the shield-bearers *lindwiʒend* (E. v. 270), the Brünnenkämpfer *byrnwiʒend* (E. v. 224, 235) and the *æscwiʒan* (E. v. 259). Besides these so variously named warriors who fought on foot we are

¹) It is worth while noting that the epithets and titles suitable to an earthly prince and warrior occur much more frequently in Passus II of Crist than in Passus I and III of the same poem: thus sinezicfa, hlaford, Aeðelinʒa Ord, beorn, Wilʒiefa, do not occur elsewhere in the poem. Moreover some appellations which are elsewhere common in the poem do not occur in Passus II e. g. Crist, Seyppend. Further the terms frea, weard, dryhten, and nerʒend occur but once each in Passus II of Crist. The most frequent appellations of the Deity in Passus II are hlaford, aðelinʒ, aðelinʒa ord, þeoden etc. Has this perhaps any significance respecting the unity or authorship of the poem?

also reminded that there was as well a body of cavalry that responded to the summons of the heralds as the Roman army gathered to defend Roman boundaries *mearh moldan trod* (E. v. 55). The battle array thus consisting of king, earls, nobles, common infantry and cavalry is furnished with hornblowers *hornboran* (E. v. 54) and war heralds *friccan* (E. v. 54) to summon the participants to and encourage them in the fight.

Before describing the fight itself we notice the armour of the warriors that the character of the fray may be the better understood. First the defensive armor. The shield was perhaps the most important piece of armour of this kind, judging from the frequency with which *bord* and *lind* occur (the last only in compounds in Elene), cf. *lindwræd* (E. v. 11), *lindwered* (E. v. 142), *lindwigend* (E. v. 270), *bordum and ordum* (E. v. 235), *rand* (E. v. 50); the latter word designates primarily the edge of the shield and then by metonomy the shield itself which is once designated as yellow *geolorand* (E. v. 118). The shield was of wood as the words *lind* and *bord* 'brett' imply. Next to the shield which served as a protection in general was the helmet of importance for the special protection of the head. This designated as *coforcumbol* (E. v. 259), *grima* (E. v. 125) *grimhelm* (E. v. 258) has been excellently discussed and described by Hans Lehmann[1]. In addition to this armour was the corselet *byrne* (E. v. 257) and the coat of mail *hildescerc* E. v. 234), *wælhlenc* (E. v. 24), which is described as *æridenc*; these together constituted the splendid war-apparel *gealolic gadserud* (E. v. 258) an expression indicating that these pieces of armour were sometimes of great splendour[2].

Of the offensive armour the sword was the most useful for the close fight; *bill(l)* E. v. 122, 257 *sweord* (E. v. 757) and *brogdenmæl* E. v. 757: the latter, the exact meaning of which is doubtful is designated as *heardecg* and was the fiery weapon of the angelic guardian of Paradise. As missiles for hurling are

[1] Hans Lehmann, Brünne and Helm im Angelsächsischen Beowulfliede; Göttinger Dissertation 1885, p. 25 ff.

[2] Cf. Lehmann p. 13 ff.: über die Brünne and his plates of Illustrations of both Helm and Brünne.

[3] Cf. Lehmann, p. 25. Also Beo. 1021 ff.

the spear *gâr* (E. v. 23. 118); *ord* (E. v. 235) used of the spear though really meaning the point. *Darraðase* (E. v. 140) is the lance with shaft of ash wood. The arrows are graphically called the battle-adders *hildenædran* (E. v. 141. 119) and the *flanas* which came down upon the fated folk in showers *scuras* (E. v. 117).

As the hosts assemble for the approaching contest, the din of armor and the commotion of moving hosts is accompanied by the dismal howl of the wolf as he sings the battle song *fyrdleoð aṡol* (E. v. 27); the scream of the dewy-feathered eagle also resounds as he rejoices in the prospects (E. v. 29). The terror of the hosts, conscious of their numerical inferiority to their barbarous foes, is increased by the uncanny cry of the fell raven as he mingles his voice with the sound of the horn and the trumpet call to battle (E. v. 52 f.). The king upon beholding the barbarian host is doubly terrified at their vast numbers, but is still resolute to defend his kingdom (v. 62 f.). The night brings him divine assurance of ultimate victory, and encouraged he gives command for the onset at the break of the following day. The war standard and the emblem through which the promised victory was to come are both raised and borne before the king; the trumpets resound loud before the attacking army *blade for herᵹum* (v. 110). The wolf, eagle, and raven lend their cries to increase the battle terror. Then comes the attack itself

  þær wæs borda gebrec and beorna ᵹeþrec

  heard handᵹeswinᵹ and herᵹa ȝrinᵹ (E. v. 114 f.)

The crash of shields, the throng of men, the discharge of weapons, the fall of the hosts are thus presented in short expressive clauses which themselves remind us of sword strokes. Showers of arrows fall upon the people doomed to death; the spears fly over the yellow shields into the crowd of the hostile ones; the arrows, the battle-adders, are impelled by the power of the fingers (v. 117 f.). The impetuous warriors still press on, the hostile hosts clash together, the shields break and finally hand to hand they strike in with the sword *bil indufan* (v. 122.). In the midst of the contest the standard *paf* (v. 123) is raised, the *seᵹn* i. e. the cross the sign of victory, and the song of victory resounded *siᵹeleoð ȝalen* (v. 124). The gilded helmets and the spears gleamed on the field. Many of the heathen fell on the field, others fled in hot haste as they saw the symbol of the cross raised; some perished in the flight, others narrowly escaped with their lives as they fled along the banks of the Danube. The pursuit of the Romans from early morning until late at night destroyed many more until the disaster to the barbarian host was almost complete. *lyþhwon becwom | huru herges batu eft þanon* (E. v. 142 f.).

There are in the other poems more or less desultory allusions to warfare and the incidents of hostile life. Pieces of armour are frequently mentioned, though generally it is offensive armour as the bow *bræʒdboʒa* (C. v. 765) and the arrow *stræl* (C. v. 765, 779) with its poisonous point *attres ord* (C. v. 768); the spear or dart *ʒar* (J. v. 17), the javelin for hurling *daroð* (J. v. 68) cf. Death of Byrhtnoth (v. 149), *daroð of handa fleoʒan* etc. The sword is referred to in one instance (C. v. 679). As the use of these terms is entirely figurative, it is natural that those terms should be employed which are most expressive in the figure and thus we find references to missiles such as darts and spears most frequent, since by the sudden and unexpected piercing of the dart the wily attacks of the devil are more accurately portrayed than by the hand to hand stroke of the sword and not because the sword was a less common or less important part of the offensive equipment.

The noise of the fiends that assail Guthlac is likened to the shout of an army *herecirm* (G. v. 872); the threats held over Juliana are called war-terror *hildewoman* (J. v. 136); the piercing of murderous arrows *wælpilum* (G. v. 1127) typifies the violence of Guthlac's pain; and the increasing severity of his last day's agony is powerfully represented as the piercing of the heart with showers of flying darts *hildescurum flacor flanþracu* (G. v. 1116 f.). The warrior of the Lord must stand against the showers of missiles *wið flanþræce* (J. v. 384)[1]. The siege of the heart as described by the devil to Juliana, the Anglosaxon poet represents as the

---

[1] This adaptation of the language to the Ags. way of thinking and interpreting through the application of literary figures in vs 1117, 1127, 1259, of Guthlac, relative to war has been pointed out by Lefèvre, Anglia Bd. VI, S. 229.

siege and capture of a city (J. v. 398 ff. First a careful survey of the defences, then an opening of the wall-gate through strategy and finally an entrance to the tower itself is obtained *bið se torr þyrel inʒonʒ ʒeopenud* and the missile discharge follows. In the same manner in Crist v. 758 ff. the representation of the strife between the good and the evil naturally falls into description of an Anglosaxon fight in which our attention is called to the terrible dart shower, the cruel wounds, the drawn bow, the bitter arrow, the sudden shot, the shielding and the treacherous weapon stroke. In Crist 558—585 the poet's mind seems to have been upon some actual victorious compaign of his own acquaintance undertaken for the adjustment of an old feud; the besieging party deprives the besieged of the tribute *ʒafol* which had of yore been unjustly exacted; the oppressor is overcome and imprisoned; those who had previously been captured are rescued and the besiegers take leave of the enemy's city *feonda byriʒ* with a rich mass of booty *huða mæste* and return amid their own hosts to their own city, rejoicing in victory, having established a lasting peace.

5. DOMESTIC AND OTHER RELATIONS.

A feeling of strong family attachment and high regard for the ties of relationship is evident wherever these relations are mentioned in the poems. Likewise a high appreciation of an honorable and lofty lineage may be inferred from several expressions referring directly to this. Mary addressing Joseph (C. v. 164 f. is careful to call him child of Jacob *Iacobes bearn* and relation of David the famous king *mæʒ Davides mæran cyninʒes*. Mary's relationship to David is also emphasized (C. v. 191). Christ is repeatedly called a noble or free-born child *freo-bearn* (C. v. 223, 643, 788). Affricanus urges his daughter to yield to the solicitations of Heliseus on the ground that he is nobler than she *æðelra* (J. v. 101) — a direct indication of the worth attached to social rank and position of which no trace is found in the poet's source.

In many instances where the Latin offers either no incentive to refer to domestic or friendly relations, or at most only a suggestion of them the poet inserts and expands in such a manner as to express considerable on these themes; thus in G. v. 840 ff.)

and 955 ff. and in J. v. 93 ff. as in several other instances which we shall have occasion to mention, this is the case. The relation of friendship between Guthlac and his servant is strongly expressed where the source gives no occasion for it.

We notice first the closest domestic relation, that of husband and wife. The relation is expressed by *sinhiwan* (G. v. 823), a strong word meaning those members of a house-hold which are joined for all time; the term is more often used in our own poems of the relation between soul and body, two companions inseparably united for this world but whose connection is dissolved at death.

            . . . . þeah his lic and ᵹæst
 hyra somwiste sinhiwan tu
 deore ᵹedælden   G. v. 911 f.

(Cf. also J. v. 697 ff.). Almost a typical mutual esteem permeates the dialogue between Joseph and Mary (C. v. 164 ff.). Although ostensibly the husband had cause, the most flagrant that could exist, to exhibit feelings of a violent and angry character, his words are tempered with forbearance and sorrow, and are reciprocated by Mary with due consolation, exculpating him from all fault. The most common word for husband is *wer* (G. v. 821, 957, J. v. 103). *Idys* is perhaps best translated wife or sponse (G. v. 956); the word has the general meaning, woman, as well. Eve gave the bitter drink to her sweet husband *hyre swæsum were* (G. v. 957). *Bryd* is used sometimes in the sense of sponsa (J. v. 41), sometimes in the sense of uxor (G. v. 812); *brydᵹuma* in the sense of sponsus (J. v. 100). The custom of ring wearing as a special token of betrothal[1] is alluded to in the expression *beaᵹu bræden*. The *witᵹifta* (J. v. 38) alludes to the old Germanic custom[2] of the betrothed girl bringing to her future husband at the marriage a certain dowry given by the girl's father. Juliana v. 38 ff. seems to refer directly to an Anglosaxon wedding, to the adorning of the bride and her escort to the house of the bridegroom *femnan ᵹeᵹyrede bryd to bolde* (Cf. J. v. 111). The terms for conjugal affection are various and expressive *lufu* (C.

---

[1] Grimm, Deutsche Rechtsalterthümer S. 177, 178, 432.
[2] Ibid. S. 429.

v. 167), *friʒu* (C. v. 419, 37, J. v. 103), *mæʒlufu* J. v. 70, *freondrædeu* (J. v. 71, 107, 220) Conjugal affection felt for the wife is tersely expressed as *brydlufu* (J. v. 114).

Almost the only opportunity that the source offers him for speaking of parental and filial affection the poet has considerably expanded, thus filia mea dulcissima Juliana lux oculorum meorum he has transferred to his own language

    þu eart dohter min   seo dyreste
    and seo sweteste   in sefan minum
    anʒe for corðan   minra eaʒna leoht
    Juliana.   (J. v. 93 ff.)

In the discourse of Sachius to his son (E. v. 111 f.) fili is translated *min sunu sunu* (v. 447) and farther on the son is addressed by the father as *hæleð min se leofa* (E. v. 510), and the pater is *min sunu fæder* (E. v. 517.) The son is again addressed as *hyse leofesta* (E. v. 523). These verbal references while not very decisive evidence of family attachment are at least indicative of the same. The relationship of Helen to her son the emperor Constantine is generally represented as that of an obedient and devoted subject rather than as kin and mother.

The only allusions to fraternal affection are those in the message of Guthlac to his sister; and here, as the deviation from the source is very slight, no more can be said than that whatever deviation there is, is on the side of greater expression of feeling than the original exhibits. G. v. 1152 ff. has no Latin equivalent. The references to Guthlac's sister are indicative of the high esteem in which woman was held; Beccelin addresses her as glory's dear virgin *wuldres wynmæʒ* (v. 1319) the dearest of maids *leofast mæʒða* (v. 1350).

Friendship and fidelity are nowhere else so vividly depicted in the Cynewulfian poems as in the relation of the servant Beccelin to Guthlac his master; and perhaps nowhere else in Anglosaxon poetry is such exalted reverence and unbounded devotion represented as here[1]. Heinzel has shown that the poet in G. v.

---

[1] Heinzel, Quellen und Forschungen über den Styl der Altgermanischen Poesie S. 44.

1020 ff., 1309 ff., and 1319 ff. has incorporated material entirely his own[1]. Lefévre[2] very properly adds references to v. 981 ff. and 1170 ff. as being independent of the source. The five passages indicated relate to the sorrow and grief felt by Beccelin upon his realization (1) of his master's sickness (v. 981 ff.), (2) upon his assurance of his approaching death (v. 1020 ff.), (3) upon receiving the message for his (Guthlac's) sister (v. 1170 ff.), (4) upon his arrival and delivery of the sad tidings as he had been commissioned to do (v. 1309 and 1319 ff.). The devotion to and the interest felt in his lord's welfare is such that the realization of the sickness affects the servant greatly

                                him þæt inȝefeol
heﬁȝ æt heortan,   hyȝesorȝe wæȝ,
micle modceare.   v. 981 f.

The description of intense feeling is perhaps strongest in (v. 1309 f.): as the servant set out to carry the sad news to his lord's sister. Sorrow hot at the heart, sad thoughts, a grievous mind troubled him who had left behind his lord, robbed of life, his dear friend; poignantly the sound of his weeping warned him, a flood of tears welled forth, the hot cheek-drops, and in his breast he bore great heart-sorrow etc. The whole passage is expressive of the most poignant grief at the loss to himself and of the most lofty respect and ardent love for the departed one.

Sarrazin in his skillful presentation of the features of Cynewulfian poetry which are common to the Beowulf poem as well, has called attention to the similarities in the descriptions of the deaths of Guthlac and Beowulf, and also to the similarities in the descriptions of the sorrow of Beccelin as compared with that of Wiȝlaf, Beowulf's relation and faithful companion[3]. A general resemblance in the description of the sorrow of the two friends is not to be denied and yet it seems to me that this distinction should be clearly made. Wiȝlaf's sorrow is that of a devoted subject for his master, that

---

[1] Heinzel, S. 44.
[2] Lefévre, Anglia Bd. VI. Das Altenglische Gedicht vom heiligen Guthlac. Lefévre has justly objected to the statement of Heinzel that v. 1020 f. is the poet's own, as there is in his source a corresponding passage of less extent.
[3] Sarrazin, Beowulf and Kynewulf, Anglia Bd. IX, S. 547.

of a warrior for his war-leader. He thinks of Beowulf as the spender of rings, of helms, swords, coats of mail etc. as he met his devoted followers in the *beorsele* (B. 2636): In the fray Wiʒlaf's master is the man of bold deeds, the terrible, destructive warrior, yielding to nothing and making all succumb to himself, and as such Wiʒlaf, a devoted follower of Beowulf's own choosing, seems ever to think of him. Beccelin on the other hand is not drawn to his master out of a warrior's admiration for heroic deeds or gigantic strength, nor out of gratitude for war-presents received in the mead-hall but rather because of Guthlac's spiritual excellencies. He thinks of Guthlac as a friend, as a father even, the true companion, the dearest of men; one whose companionship was most highly prized and whose loss was an irreparable calamity.

The servant in relation to Guthlac is called *ombehtþeʒn* (G. v. 973, 1119, 1268), *maʒu* (v. 983), *þeʒn* (v. 1087), with slight if any difference of meaning. Terms significant of intimate friendship and fraternal affection applied to the servant are *min þæt swæse bearn* (G. v. 1139), *wine min* (v. 1200), *leofast monna* (v. 1231), *breowum ʒeside* (v. 1269), all strong expressions indicative of the lord's high appreciation of his servants love and companionship *lufan þinre and ʒeferscype* (G. v. 1231 f.. Guthlac on the other hand in relation to the servant is the *mondryhten* (v. 1024, 1124, 980); as addressed by the servant himself, he is the friendly lord *winedryhten min* (v. 984, 1175), *fæder* (v. 985), the protector of friends *freonda hleo* (v. 985), the dearest prince *þeoden leofesta* (v. 887), noble lord *freodryhten* (v. 991), lord *hlaford* (v. 1026), the dearest of men *hæleða leofast* (v. 1176), Joy of earls *eorla wyn* (v. 1179) and *fæder frofor min* (v. 1184), *frea min* (v. 1195), *hlaford min* (v. 1331).

The servant's message to the sister herself is a beautiful tribute to the high esteem in which constancy in friendship was held by the Anglosaxon (v. 1322 ff.). A tribute to strong family attachment is also yielded by the poet in v. 1154 ff. which adds considerable to the original respecting the pleasure of Guthlac's sister's companionship constituting one of the joys of heaven: in a passage entirely the poet's own the same is referred to again in G. v. 1345 ff.

Having noticed political and social relations so far as they are found in the poems, as I believe, I wish to note next some references to the seat of different intellectual and emotional impressions, references to the individual man, to men in general and to different occupations and customs.

In addition to what has been said respecting friendship and emotions we may notice the names given to the seat of these impressions. For heart was the general name *heortan* (C. v. 174, J. v. 239, G. v. 982, *hyge* E. v. 685); this word Grimm connects with the name of the wise bird Huginn by which the highest god obtained information[1]. *Mod* (C. v. 1601, J. v. 39, G. v. 1041) is used also of the heart as seat of thought and emotion. *Sefa* (C. v. 412, G. v. 938) means mind; *hreðer* (C. v. 539, G. v. 910) is the breast as seat of the emotions and *hreðerloca* G. v. 1237) is the breast (*hreðer*) enclosure; *hreðercofa* is also the *hreðer* apartment; *ferð* (C. v. 1331, J. v. 270, G. v. 985) is mind, soul or spirit and *ferðloca* (J. v. 239, 279) is the enclosure, the 'Verschluss' of the *ferð*. Almost synonymous with these are *breost* (C. v. 341), *modsefa* (J. v. 72) and *breostsefa* (C. v. 510). The *breosthord* may be either the heart itself, or life or the thoughts whose seat was located in the breast.

The terms descriptive of the body are especially poetic, often metaphorical in character. The Anglosaxon distinguished sharply in his terminology between the body simply and the body united with the spirit *gæst* or soul *sawel*. The body apart from life is most often called *lichoma* (C. v. 755, J. v. 115, G. v. 1073); *lic* is also found; *hra* may be body either living or dead (C. v. 14); further designating the body are bone-enclosure *banloca* (C. v. 769, J. v. 476, G. v. 914) or the bone-apartment *bancofa* (G. v. 927) or the bone-vessel *banfæt* (G. v. 1166, 1239) — — *banloca* is the favorite expression in Guthlac. The body is also *licfæt* (G. v. 1063), bone-house *banhus* (G. v. 1314), soul-house *sawelhus* (G. v. 1003), the tenement of the soul *hus* (E. v. 880). Alluding to the flesh rather than the bone the body is a flesh-covering *flæschoma* (C. v. 1298, J. v. 489, G. v. 1004); as something

[1] Grimm, Vorrede zu Andreas und Elene XXXIX.

which shall return to the earth it is the earth-hord *greathord* (G. v. 1240).

The life itself as a distinct something is the treasure of the body *lichord* (G. v. 929), the *feorhhord* (G. v. 1117) and the *gæst* or *sawel*. The comparison of the two soul and body to the married inmates of the same house *sinhiwan* has already been referred to. I give here a complete list of references to the places in the Cynewulfian poems where the two are spoken of together, generally with reference to their living together on earth or to their separation from each other at death: C. v. 597 f., 777 f., 1327 f., 1580 f.; J. v. 669 f., 699 f., 714 f.; G. v. 940, 901, 810, 1062 f., 1149 f., 1272 f., 1237 f.; E. v. 889; F. A. v. 37, 83.

The poetical designations of the individual man are rich in variety and descriptiveness. I mention the more important of them. To the sea-loving Anglosaxon, man is an ocean-dweller *sundbuend* (C. v. 73, 221), or described from his mode of habitation he is a citadel-dweller *burgsittende* (C. v. 339); other expressions are: those endowed with speech *reordberend* (C. v. 278, 381), also *corðwaru* (C. v. 582, 723), *corðbuend* (C. v. 422, 1279) *þeodbuend* (C. v. 616, 1372), *foldbuend* (C. v. 868, G. v. 911); *gæstberende* (C. v. 1600), the offspring of the earth *corðan tudder* (C. v. 688).

We learn little from these poems of how the Anglosaxon spent his time, how he was occupied apart from his employment in war or on the sea of which occupations mention is made elsewhere in this essay. In Elene those are spoken of who made the cross according to the emperor's directions, and there were those mechanics also who were able to set it with precious stones and to adorn it with gold (E. v. 1022 ff.). Those who were most skillful in stone-cutting were commanded by Helen to build the church upon the spot where the cross was found. References to the bishop *biscop*, the prophet *witga* and the counsellor are of course found in poems of this character. In Crist however there is one passage still (v. 666 ff.) which is very interesting in this connection, even if it does show some similarities with the Biblical passage 1 Cor. 12, 7—10, and was in all likelihood suggested by some thoughts in Gregory's twenty-ninth homily. That the poet has in mind occupations with which he is familiar is shown by his enthusiastic reference to sea and war-life. One can sing and speak many things *se mæg ealfela singan and secgan*: here we may readily think that the poet has the scop in mind: perhaps recalling his own earlier career; another can play the harp skillfully *hearpan stirgan gleobeam gretan*; this may well designate the gleeman or minstrel whose presence upon festive occasions was not only agreeable but quite indispensable; a third can teach, interpret the Divine Law *sum mæg godcunde / recean rihte æ*; another can tell the course of the stars *ryne tungla secgan* is an astrologer; another is a copyist — can write well the spoken word, *mæg searolice wordewide writan*; another is a warrior, another a seaman and yet another applies his talents to the preparation of weapons *mæg styled sweord, wæpen geyrcean*; another has special knowledge of the topography of the country *con wongsa bigongs weges widgielle*; another has special physical activity and skill, can climb the lofty tree *mæg heanne beam .... gestigan*. The lines whence these references have been taken, though doubtless suggested by the source above referred to, cause us involuntarily to recall different occupations of the middle ages: the profession of the scop and gleeman, the teacher and monk, the seaman and warrior, the astrologer, the weaponsmith and the athlete.

I have already referred to the custom of drinking in the mead-hall so often referred to in Beowulf, and to the *dream* as an enjoyment which those barred from heaven may not have. I shall mention now several other references to drinking where the poet discloses, inadvertently perhaps, phases of Anglosaxon life. These references are in Juliana and Guthlac and are independent of his source. The poet makes the devil say (J. v. 183 ff.) that one of his ways of working evil is by causing men drunk with beer *beore druncne* to renew old grudges, and by lending to them from the cup such enmity that in the wine-hall they perished by the sword-stroke. The temptation, yielded to by Eve and by her set before Adam, with all its malignant consequences is compared to a bitter drink *þone bitran drync* (G. v. 840), a potion which each one of the human race must drink because of old the young bride drank to her husband *byrelade bryd geong*. The same idea is presented in (G. v. 955 f.): and the inherited sin which no one may escape is compared to a draught of misery, a cup of death *þone bleatan dryne............ deopum deaðweʒes*. These allusions and comparisons bear with them the suggestion at least, that within the range of the poet's own observation excessive drinking was at times indulged in and carried even to the extremes of drunkenness and baleful quarrels.

IV. NATURE.

It were perhaps superfluous to preface what I shall have to say under the above heading by any attempt to explain why the manifestations of nature, and especially the sea, with which I shall be principally occupied in this chapter, worked so powerfully upon the mind of the poet. A people whose island home was found only after tedious sailing over the roughest of seas, and no corner of whose island was more than a few days' journey from a coast which affords almost all degrees of rugged and picturesque scenery, and where ocean wave, tide and current beat ceaselessly, must of necessity have had an intimate acquaintance with and certain love for the ocean and the various experiences of ocean life. The literature of the Anglosaxons bears all marks of this familiarity with the ocean and all that concerns it, whether it be attractive or repulsive. An interesting and valuable study of the descriptions of natural scenery in the old Germanic poetry is that of Lüning [1]. The subject is looked at in all of its aspects. The sea has been quite exhaustively treated by Merbach [2], who has studied his subject in the whole field of the poetical Anglosaxon literature.

The allusions to the sea in the Cynewulfian poems — with the exception of the description of Helen's voyage — like the references to war, are desultory and apt to appear as the overflow from a mind stored with a rich sea vocabulary which is seizing

---

[1] Lüning, Die Natur, ihre Auffassung und poetische Verwendung in der Altgermanischen und mittelhochdeutschen Epik bis zum Abschluss der Blütezeit. Zürich, 1889.

[2] Hans Merbach, Das Meer in der Dichtung der Angelsachsen. Breslauer Dissertation, 1885.

every opportunity to express itself upon a subject of which it is especially fond.

Considering the number of references to the sea, the names for it are very numerous and vary according to the impressions it made upon the mind. Many of these designations are very poetical in themselves: they are often suggested by some peculiarity of the sea itself or its inhabitants. Of frequent occurence is *sæ* (C. v. 677, 1145, E. v. 240); other expressions are *flod, pl. flodas; lagu*, the rune, may designate generally the waters: *lagufloð* (C. v. 851, J. v. 674); *holm* (C. v. 856, J. v. 112); *holmþracu* (C. v. 678, E. v. 727) "ungestüme See"); *deop gelad* (C. v. 857, G. v. 1266); *hreone hryeg* (C. v. 859); *yð* (C. v. 855, 1168, E. v. 239) designates the wave really but is used often in the plural to denote sea; *wæg* (C. v. 981, J. v. 680, E. v. 230); *stream* (J. v. 481, E. v. 1200) designates the sea as a moving body of water in contrast with a lake of standing water (*sæ mere standað*, Beow. 1363); the same word designates the Danube *lagostream* (E. v. 137); *ealıstream* (C. v. 1168, J. v. 673); *yðfaru* (J. v. 178); *mereflod* (J. v. 480). As a thoroughfare, the sea was named the *merestræt* (E. v. 242) and the swan's road *swanrad* (J. v. 675). It is further *egestream* (E. v. 241) and *earhgeblond* (E. v. 239) 'meeresgemisch', and *fifelwæg* (E. v. 237). Grimm[2] connects this last word with the Old North *fimbul* in *fimbulul* etc. and derives therefrom the idea of murmuring, rustling; Merbach[3]) cites Beow. v. 104 *fifel-cynnes eard*, the dwelling place of monsters, as the meaning here seems, and so reaches the conclusion that a general meaning for *fifel* is 'rauschendes ungeheuer' or 'wasserungetüm', so that the meaning of *fifelwæg* here is 'die flut der seeungetümer'. *Geofon*[4] is used as a general name for ocean. Designating the sea as something closed to man, as a stronghold which must be conquered before it could be made serviceable is the expression *lagufæsten* (E. v. 249). *Brim* (E. v. 253, 971) and *sund* (E. v. 228) are of frequent occurrence in poetry. As a highway and a home for animal life, where birds dive after

---

[1]) Zupitza, Glossar zur dritten Auflage v. Elene.
[2]) Andreas and Elene, S. 147.
[3]) Merbach, S. 8.
[4]) Cf. Müller in Haupt's Zeitschrift, I, 95.

prey or for the purpose of bathing, the sea is a *baðweg* (E. v. 244). Cf. *fiscesbæð*, An. v. 293)¹).

The foregoing names themselves are often descriptive of the Anglosaxon's mental pictures of the sea. But he was not content to decribe it by pictorial names alone. He added a list of adjectives which aid the clear expression of his conception. He viewed the sea as occupying an extensive bed *on sidne grund* (C. v. 1165), as being extensive *sidne* (C. v. 853), *se brada* (C. v. 1145), *sæs sidne faðm* (E. v. 728), and salty *sealtne* (C. v. 679) and deep *deop* (C. v. 857) and rough *reone* (J. v. 481) and windy *windige* (C. v. 856) and cold *cald* (C. v. 852) and foamy *famige* (E. v. 237) and high *ofer heanne holm* (E. v. 982) and dangerous *freene* (C. v. 854) and surging *wæges wylm* (J. v. 680) *yða swengas* (E. v. 239) and of enormous waves *yða ofermæta* (C. v. 855). The shores were either high precipitous, rocky cliffs *heah cleofu* (C. v. 979), steadfast barriers *stið and stædfast staðelas* (C. v. 984), or the low sandy beach *sandlond* (G. v. 1309), and these constitute its boundaries *clomme* (C. v. 1146). The shore is often called *staeð* (E. v. 232, 227 etc.), the land bordering on the water without any specification as to the character of the coast.

It is pertinent also to speak of the boat²); and here we have to do with a set of expressions quite as numerous as those for the sea itself, nor are they less poetical. We have the simple expressions *scip* (J. v. 672) and *bat* (G. v. 1302), and *ceol* keel (C. v. 852, 862, E. v. 250) which by metonomy designates the ship. *Wudu* is used frequently in combination with other words to denote the ship, thus *sundwudu* (C. v. 677) and *flotwudu* (C. v. 854), *brimwudu* (E. v. 241, G. v. 1305). Beownlf furnishes the expression *sæwudu* (v. 226).

Especially striking is the personification of the ship as a horse *sundhengest* (C. v. 853, 863) and *wæghengest* (G. v. 1303; E. v. 236) *faroðhengest* (E. v. 226). Combinations with *mearh* are the following *yðmearh* (C. v. 864), *lagumearh* (G. v. 1306) and *sæmearh* (E. v. 245). Merbach (p. 35) notes that this comparison of the boat to a horse is a point at which the sea and

¹) Cf. Lüning, p. 89 ff.
²) Ibid. p. 96 ff.

war-life of the Anglosaxon touch: wie der Krieger auf ungestümem Streitrosse zum Kampfe ausreitet, so der Seefahrer auf unbändigem Wogenrosse zum wilden Streit mit Wind und Wellen. As a floater the boat is the *wægflota* (E. v. 246) and the *hærnflota* (G. v. 1307) and *brimpisa* (E. v. 238). Grimm[1]) connects *pisa* with *bys*, Gerausch, and so derives the meaning Flutdurchrauscher for *brimpisa*: in favor of this meaning is its use with *bronte* foaming and *famige* of the preceding line; related to this is *wæterpiswa* (G. v. 1303). Other names are *bord* (E. v. 238) which alludes to the hull of the Ship as is seen from its use with *yða swengas*. Kent's conjecture[2]) that we have here a figurative epithet drawn from the use of the shield in battle seems to me most reasonable. As the shield was the recipient of the assailing weapons so the hull of the ship battled with the assailing waves. *Hringedstefnn* (E. v. 248) like *ceol* is an instance of the use of pars pro toto and alludes to rings on the prow by which the boats could be made fast, or as seems to me just as likely — to carved decorations in ring shape on the prow of the boat[3]). From the illustrations of the Cædmon MSS one may easily obtain the conception of the *yðhofu* or home on the waves. The personification of the boat as an animal would be most natural when the prow was formed into the shape of an animal's head and the stern made to represent its tail as is the case in three of these pictures. We still have to mention the full sail *swelling* (E. v. 245) and the anchor *oncor* (E. v. 252) by which the boat was made fast *sælan* (E. v. 228).

Respecting the crews of the boats and their duties we are told nothing in these poems, as those who go on board the boats with Helen on her expedition are warriors who take with them all the equipments of soldiers. The sailor is not described; we may infer, however, from some phrases referring to the motion of the ship with what enthusiasm a voyage was undertaken and with what fearlessness — almost recklessness — the sailor betook

[1]) Andreas and Elene S. XXXIV.
[2]) Kent's Dissertation p. 54.
[3]) Cf. Illustrations to the Cædmon MS. Archaeologia XXIV. Plates LXXXVIII, LXXXIX, XC, XCI.

himself to the waves. Sailing is expressed by *lacan* (J. v. 674, C. v. 855) a word which may mean sporting, dancing (Cf. Heyne's Beow. Glossary): the voyage is the ocean-play *sundplega* (G. v. 1308). To sail is further *sundewudu drifan* (C. v. 677); *flotwudu fergen* (C. v. 854); to stir the impetuous sea *hreran holmþræce* (C. v. 678). Consistent with the comparison of the boat to a steed is the comparison of sailing to stepping *scriðan* (E. v. 237). The following lines from Guthlac 1305 ff. descriptive of the passage of a boat through the water may serve as an example of the poetic character of the references to the sea:

    Brimwudu seynde
leoht lade fus: la3umearʒ snyrede
ʒehlæsted to hyðe,   þæt se hærnflota
æfter sundplegan,   sondlond ʒespearn
ʒrond wið ʒreote.   (G. v. 1305 ff.

Especially skilful is the description of the roaring of the sailing boat as it passes through the foaming waters:

    Leton þa ofer fifelwæʒ famiʒe scriðan
    bronte brimþisan.   E. v. 237.)

The rapid succession here of words meaning roaring, murmuring, displays both the wealth of poetical expression the poet had at his disposal and also the skill with which he knew how to use it.

The poet alludes to other manifestations of nature, as well as the sea, with a heartiness which bespeaks his love for and intimacy with out-door life. He saw about him the broad[1] *brade* C. v. 992), *sidne* (C. v. 1008) and bright creation *ʒesceaft* above which was the roof of the sky *rodores hrof* (C. v. 59) or the roof of clouds *wolcna hrof* (E. v. 89). At his feet was the earth which he variously named *hruse* (C. v. 883, E. v. 218), *molde* (E. v. 55, C. v. 889), *folde* (E. v. 721, C. v. 72), *middanʒeard* (C. v. 248) made up of wide plains *wongas* (C. v. 811, E. v. 684) and furnished with mountains *beorʒum* (C. v. 968). The plains are decked with blooming flowers (G. v. 1249) and furnished with artificial and natural products which constitute the beauties or

[1] Cf. Läning, p. 220.

decorations of the landscape *londes frætwa* (G. v. 1256. 1270). The earth was also named the *foldweʒ* (G. v. 1224) and the *moldweʒ* (J. v. 334) and the *foldwonʒ* (G. v. 1300) over which was the bright expanse of the heavens with its stars [1] *torhtne mit his tunglum* (C. v. 969) resplendent with starry gems *tungolʒimmum* (C. v. 1151. 1148).

The Anglosaxon was doubtless familiar with the dense fogs that often enveloped sea and land about his coasts yet references to them in Anglosaxon poetry are extremely seldom. This has been accounted for by the conjecture [2] that the singer as well as his hearers had no appreciation in song of a theme which afforded them such opposition as neither courage or skill could overcome. We have the *misthelm* mentioned but in a figurative sense only (J. v. 470). Allusions to winds and storms are also wanting.

The sun was especially impressive among the phenomena of nature and the poet loved to set forth his risings and settings in the most poetic language, and dwelt with fervour on the gradual change from daylight to darkness and vice versa. He called the sun the gem of heaven *heofones ʒim* (G. v. 1185) and the blissful light of men *wynwondel wera* (G. v. 1186), the noble gleam *se wðela ʒleam* (G. v. 1252), the warm weather token *wedertacen wearm* (G. v. 1267). The sun and moon are often mentioned together as stars of superior magnitude and brilliancy *sunne and mona wðelast tungla* (C. v. 606) or as the candles of heaven *heofoncondelle* (C. v. 608), as holy gems *halʒa ʒimmas* (C. v. 692), the brilliant stars of heaven *hadre heofontunʒol* (C. v. 693). The setting of the sun is its gradual descent in the west *west onhylde* (G. v. 1186), where after each day's journey across the heavens it sought its seat *setlʒonʒes fus* (G. v. 1187), *setlʒonʒ sohte* (G. v. 1253).

After the disappearance of the sun the gradual coming on of darkness is beautifully described: Then the noble gleaming sought its rest, the northern sky grew dusky, dark under the

---

[1] Cf. Lüning. p. 65.
[2] Merbach, S. 22 f.
[3] Lüning, p. 58 ff.

clouds, mist spread over the world, decked it in darkness
throughout the night, hid the decorations of the land

þa se æðela glæm
setl,on,g sohte   sweare norðrodor
won under wolcum   worulde miste oferteah
þystrum biþeahte   þring niht ofer
lihte londes frætwa.   (G. v. 1252 ff.)

The Anglosaxon delighted to represent the sun as rising over
the sea as indeed was natural to him whose horizon was the point
of apparent contact of the sea with the sky quite as often as the
point of contact of the earth with the sky. The breaking of the
morning over the earth after the night in which the phenomenal
light appeared above Guthlac's dwelling is called the rustling of
the approaching day *dægredwoma* and is represented as coming
over the deep sea from the west

eastan cwom
ofer deop gelad   dægredwoma
wedertacen wearm   (G. v. 1265 ff.)

Not only the approaching light but the gloaming *æfenglome*
(G. v. 1265), the eventide[1] *æfentid* (G. v. 1188) and the darkness[2]
itself which he named the *nihthelm* (G. v. 943, E. v. 78) are
phases of nature which particularly appealed to the poet.

Besides the phenomena which shall be evident on the Last
Day are two, mentioned in Guthlac, which deserve notice because
here the poet has considerably enlarged upon the original Latin.
G. v. 1256 ff. is the decription of a miraculous light which appeared
about Guthlac's dwelling on the last night of the saints' life.
The two lines of Latin are expanded to three times that amount
of Anglosaxon. The poet's wealth of expression represents it as the
greatest of lights *leohta mæst*, which shone brilliantly *beadre scinan*,
bright over the house *beorht ofer burgsalu*, a noble gleam of glory
wuldres scima, brilliantly arrayed *scirwered*, a heavenly candle
heofonlic condel, a gleam of light before which the shadows flee
away. The other marvelous light which appeared after Guthlac's death is also beautifully described but the addition to the

[1] Lüning, p. 44 ff.
[2] Ibid. p. 49 ff.

original is here not so marked. This light is a fiery tower *fyren tor* (G. v. 1285), brighter than the sun *sunnan beorhtra* and with the splendor of noble stars *æðeltungla wlite*.

In reckoning time *winter* (E. v. 1. 633) has the signification of year. The seasons of the year are referred to: *sumeres tid* (G. v. 1247), spring *lencten* (E. v. 1226). Summer began on the 6th day after the Kalends of May.

       wæs þa lencten agan
  butan VI nihtum ær sumeres cyme
  on Maias kalendas,   (E. v. 1226)

or on the 7th of May. Reckoning the seasons at three months each we should have them beginning on the 7th of May, August, November, and February. And this division of the year makes the winter and summer solstices exactly at the middle of the winter and summer seasons respectively[1]. Time was often reckoned by nights as regards periods of 24 hours each just as by winters when reckoning in respect to periods of twelve months each; this may be seen in the lines just quoted from Elene. In numbering the days which Guthlac had to live we find *ponne seofon niht fyrstgemearces* (G. v. 1008) and *nihtrim seridon* (G. v. 1070).

Plant and animal life are practically forgotten by the poet whose attention was allured by the more awe-inspiring manifestations of the world about him. Thus, first of all the sea, the broad expanse of waters, then the heavens, the starry fields, the sun and the moon affected him mightily, and next to these the topography of the land, the rocky shores, the barriers of the restless waves, the towering mountains and extensive plains. These were the manifestations of nature that found place in his song, rather than the birds the flowers and the trees.

[1] Cf. Grimm, Andreas and Elene XXIV and 171.

LITERATURE.

The following are the principal works used in the preparation of the foregoing dissertation.
Anglosaxon Texts. As cited in Introduction.

Grimm, J. Deutsche Mythologie. Göttingen, 1844.
Grimm, J. Deutsche Rechtsalterthümer. Göttingen, 1828.
Kemble, J. M. Saxons in England. A History of the English Commonwealth till the Period of the Norman Conquest. London, 1849.
Mogk, E. Article on 'Mythologie' in Paul's Grundriss der Germanischen Philologie.
Wülker, R. P. Grundriss zur Geschichte der angelsächsischen Literatur. Leipzig, 1885.
Ten Brink. History of English Literature, Vol. I. English by Horace M. Kennedy.
Bugge. Studien über die Entstehung der nordischen Götter und Heldensagen. German by G. O. Brenner. München, 1889.
Archæologia or Miscellaneous Tracts relating to Antiquity. Published by the Society of Antiquaries at London. Vol. XXIV, 1833.
Lüning, Otto. Die Natur, ihre Auffassung und poetische Verwendung in der Altgermanischen und Mittelhochdeutschen Epik. Zürich, 1889.
Zupitza, J. Elene. Herausgegeben, Berlin, 1888. 3. Aufl.
Hoyne, M. Beowulf. 5. Aufl. Paderborn und Münster, 1888.
Kent, C. W. Teutonic Antiquities in Andreas and Elene. Halle, 1887.
Rau, Max. Germanische Alterthümer in der angelsächsischen Exodus. Leipzig, 1889.
Köhler. Germanische Alterthümer im Beowulf. Pfeiffer's Germania. Bd. 13.
Merbach, Hans. Das Meer in der Dichtung der Angelsachsen. Breslau, 1885.

The various articles respecting Cynewulf and the Cynewulfian Poetry that have appeared in the *Anglia;* referred to elsewhere in the dissertation.

VITA.

I, Milo B. Price, was born Sep. 10th 1867 near Newark, Licking County, Ohio, U. S. A., as sixth son of Thos. D. Price. I was reared in the Evangelical Faith and am a member of the Baptist Church. My early education was obtained at the District School of my home neighborhood. At seventeen years of age I entered the Preparatory School of Granville College at Granville, Ohio. The Preparatory Course of three years and the College Course of four years were successfully completed and I was graduated as Bachelor of Arts in 1892. The following year I spent in Chicago as student of the University of Chicago and as tutor in a Preparatory School of the University. In the autumn of 1893, I entered the University of Leipzig where I have spent five semesters. During these semesters I have heard lectures by the Professors and Doctors, Wülker, Sievers, Marcks, Volkelt, Lamprecht, Elster and Holz. I have been a member of Professor Wülker's English Seminar and have taken part in the exercises in interpretation.

To all of the above named gentlemen I am deeply indebted, but in an especial manner to Professors Wülker, Marcks and Volkelt for many valuable suggestions in regard to my work at the University.

www.ingramcontent.com/pod-product-compliance
Lightning Source LLC
Chambersburg PA
CBHW020252090426
42735CB00010B/1890